# *I'M TRAVELING AS FAST AS I CAN*
## A Travelogue of Humorous Stories and Visual Vignettes

# GORDON SNIDER

# I'M TRAVELING AS FAST AS I CAN
## A Travelogue of Humorous Stories and Visual Vignettes

Helm Publishing

For information address:
Helm Publishing
Treasure Island FL  33706

www.publishersdrive.com

ISBN 978-0-9850488-4-6
Printed in the United States of America

# OTHER BOOKS BY GORDON SNIDER

## Non-Fiction

Winning Marketing Strategies

How to Become a Killer Competitor

## Fiction

Sigourney's Quest

The Separatist

The Hypnotist

Venice Lost

The Origamist (to be released next year as a sequel to The Hypnotist)

## DEDICATION

Many of these stories would not have happened without my travel partner in life, so I dedicate this book to Fe, my wife, whose pioneer spirit made this book possible.

# TABLE OF CONTENTS

# CHAPTER ONE
## *Been There, Done That*

My wife and I had been sitting on the airport tarmac in Tbilisi, Georgia, for nearly an hour, and my palms had grown moist enough to water a pot of geraniums. Not that airline delays were unusual in the old Soviet Union. In fact, the only thing more mysterious than the departure times of our flights was the drinks offered by our frowning flight attendants as they made their cursory rounds down the aisles. The glasses contained a brown liquid that looked so forbidding, we dared not drink it.

It was the local travelers who were jammed into every available seat around us that tipped me off something was amiss. Their placid demeanors had been replaced by worried murmurs and uneasy glances towards the rear of our Aeroflot jet. I tried to make eye contact with one of the grim-faced stewardesses for reassurance that everything was alright but received an icy stare for my trouble. That didn't surprise me. I'd been on enough Aeroflot flights to know there would be no information forthcoming from the Russian pilots or those unsmiling flight attendants. They saw no reason to keep the passengers informed. So, we sat in our uncomfortable seats, unmoving, and patiently waited.

The effect was claustrophobic. I was squeezed into a middle seat not much bigger than a child's car seat with my wife, Fe, by the window and a hulking man in a rumpled suit on the aisle. The body heat from so many trapped passengers was rapidly raising the temperature inside the cabin from merely uncomfortable to a level more akin to roasting chestnuts. At any moment, I expected the walls of the plane to close in and suffocate me.

It was time, I decided, to take some action, so I rose from my seat and squeezed past my fellow traveler into the aisle. This prompted a frown from the nearest flight attendant, who advanced towards me with a firm "nyet" etched on her face. Before she could reach me, however, I walked far enough down the aisle to see three crew members struggling to secure the rear door of our aging aircraft. The scene did little to lower my anxiety level, and my panic meter quickly rose from distressed to scared-out-of-my-wits when a steward strolled past me holding a pair of scissors and a roll of electrical tape in his beefy hands. Using electrical tape to secure an airplane's door might have seemed like a reasonable solution to the Aeroflot crew, but their problem-solving skills left me wondering why my wife and I had ever decided to visit the Soviet Union in the first place.

I hastily returned to my seat, but not because of the flight attendant's "nyet." Fe and I had to decide what action to take. We discussed abandoning that leg of our journey in favor of another flight, but we both knew that wasn't a very practical option. The year was 1987, and while perestroika might have been in full bloom, the Soviet government still subsidized air travel for the empire's far-flung populations, making domestic Aeroflot flights the equivalent of flying trains and buses. Most flights were booked days or weeks in advance, and everything except live chickens and goats was brought onboard and either jammed between the legs of passengers or stored in the aisles.

On a previous flight from Samarkand, Uzbekistan, the man

seated in the aisle next to me had wedged a great, rough-hewn bag of melons between his legs. Once again, I'd been confined to the middle seat, which seemed to be my fate on those Aeroflot flights. My neighbor had been just as bulky as the one seated next to me now, only he had worn flowing robes and smelled of onions and too many nights in the desert without bathing.

Most of our flights included at least one potentially lethal object left unattended in the aisle (on this flight it was a bicycle), and most flights were accompanied by flies, which seemed to enjoy air travel as much as our fellow travelers. Our current flight out of Tbilisi was an exception, however. The flies had been replaced by large wasps that buzzed around the cabin's interior with the agility of WWII fighter pilots. I supposed they had boarded through that uncooperative back door and were attracted to all the food being transported by the passengers.

Speaking of food, we did receive some tired, boiled chicken on two legs of our journey, but on most segments nothing was offered except that mysterious, brown liquid. We were generally parched and famished by the time we reached our next destination.

But none of those inconveniences mattered now. It was decision time. We had to choose between the adhesive merits of electrical tape at 30,000 feet and running for our lives. Not only were the seat belts hardly functional, I was pretty sure there would be no oxygen masks tumbling from the overhead compartments to rescue us when the back door blew off. Our only alternative was to abandon ship and face the prospect of several more days in Tbilisi without a hotel reservation. In the end, our practical natures overcame our doubts, and we placed our trust in the steward and his electrical tape. We crossed ourselves and said a few "Hail Marys" as the plane finally sped down the runway and lifted into the black, unyielding night. Miraculously, the door held fast, and passengers, melons, bicycle, and wasps all landed safely in Leningrad (now St. Petersburg). We were tired, jittery, and hungry by the time we arrived. Not to mention thirsty. Fear works up a real good thirst. Had we been cats, we would just have used up one of our nine lives.

3

That experience is the perfect segue to the question: why were we so willing to subject ourselves to such mental and physical discomforts just to spend a few days or weeks traveling someplace where they may not even have an espresso machine? I'm not including domestic travel in this question, even though there are places in the U.S. that are bound to feel foreign to many of us, and we've all heard the horror stories of flights sitting on the tarmac for hours on end. Nor am I referring to the annual ritual of visiting relatives. Such trips can be rewarding, but they don't expand our horizons or take our breath away. I'm talking about foreign countries where the language, food, customs, culture, and infrastructure often leave us wondering if we're still on the same planet.

The trick is to adjust to our unfamiliar surroundings and to make the most of those unexpected surprises that seem to pop up at the darnedest times. Some of us deal with them better than others, but if I had to pick a country that excels at this, it would be the Australians.

Here's an example. A number of years ago, I was on a business trip to the Philippines, and I had just sat down in the lobby of the famous Manila Hotel for a meeting with one of the hotel managers when two bus loads of vacationers came pouring through the front door. The manager told me they were Australian salesmen who had earned sales awards in the form of free vacations for themselves and their wives. I had run into enough Aussies in my world travels to know they were a fun-loving bunch, and I suspected the hotel was in for a rowdy good time. Little did I realize just how rowdy things would get. I flew home the next day, and while I was still in flight, I learned that an attempted military coup was in progress at the Manila Hotel. I had missed the coup by only a few hours! It was a chaotic time in the Philippines' history. Marcos had been deposed, and Corazon Aquino was president. Many factions were trying to wrestle control of the country away from her, and attempted coups were about as common as those flies on Aeroflot. They generally never lasted more than a day or two and few shots were fired.

My first reaction at the news was a sigh of relief. Thank goodness I'd left the hotel before the rebels arrived. Then I thought about those poor Australian salesmen and their wives. They had looked giddy at the prospect of spending a week frolicking in the sun. Now, news reports were describing panicked tourists escaping through the kitchen ahead of the marauding rebels, who had stormed into the hotel with rifles at the ready. I visualized terrified Aussies trapped in their rooms, their vacations ruined.

Months later, I returned to the Philippines and held another meeting at the Manila Hotel. Evidence of the damage caused by the rebels was still visible, and my thoughts turned, once more, to those unfortunate couples.

"What ever happened to the Australians I saw checking in the last time I was here?" I asked the manager. "Were they able to escape? I hope their vacations weren't completely ruined."

"Heavens no," the manager replied with a chuckle. "They had a marvelous time. It was the Americans we were sneaking out of the hotel. The Australians were all down in the bar drinking with the rebels!"

Leave it to the Aussies, I thought, to turn an attempted coup into a party! It turned out the media had overplayed the incident, and none of the hotel guests were hurt. In fact, after drinking up the bar's liquor, the rebels bid farewell to their new friends and returned to their barracks. The Aussies continued their vacation without missing a beat.

Having a good time is certainly one reason to visit other countries, but travel is personal for each of us, and our motivations vary as distinctively as the finger prints we leave on our daily lives. Personally, I have been seeking foreign adventures for over thirty years, and memories of my first trips still glisten with the glow of dew drops catching the early morning light. But this still begs the question. Why do it? Part of the answer lies in those motivations, the reasons we travel. It's always dangerous to generalize, but here are a few categories of travelers that I have observed over the years. See if you recognize a friend or relative in a category or two, or perhaps yourself!

**Been There, Done That:** These are people who travel to places so they can say they have been there. They love to count the number of countries they have visited, show photographs of their latest destinations, and share their souvenirs like trophies. When your path crosses theirs in some foreign land, they can drop the names of exotic locations faster than you can say Borobudur (an ancient temple located in Indonesia). See, I'm guilty of this from time-to-time myself. Perhaps we're all a little guilty of name dropping if we include travel in the fabric of our lives, but these people do it to a fare-thee-well!

**Shop Until You Drop:** Historical sights and scenic surroundings act as backdrops to stores filled with shoes, clothing, handbags, and souvenirs. These people have more stamina than Himalayan trekkers. They march from shop to shop in city after city with a purpose not unlike Sherman's march through the South. Their goal is complete conquest of every buying opportunity, and they are not satisfied until their arms, their loved ones' arms, and any available vehicles are filled to the brim with packages, boxes, and bags. Of course, they always bring back a T-shirt or some other gift for everyone. Don't you just hate that? I immediately feel guilty as sin, because I'm usually too busy exploring some jungle or back alley to think about shopping for souvenir gifts.

**Fart and Go:** My sister-in-law in Germany coined this expression to describe people who only stop in each city long enough for a quick peek, then off they go again. A half-day city tour and an afternoon of souvenir shopping are usually all they need to satisfy their curiosity. Larger cities, say Rome or Paris, might hold their attention for an extra day or two, but typically it's "twenty-four hours and we're out of here." A normal trip to Europe, for example, would include five capitals in ten days. As my wife's sister would say, "they stop to fart and then they go!" They have great potential to become Been There Done Thats.

**Historians:** These people read everything they can get their hands on about each destination before traveling there, then listen carefully to every word offered by the tour guides and lecturers at important ruins, museums, and landmarks. They can rattle off facts with amazing clarity and confidence, which can be a bit intimidating. My father was a historian who could pull the most obscure information out of his hat on any of the places he had visited. Of course, it helped that he had a photographic memory. I am most definitely not a historian. In fact, I generally abandon Fe to listen patiently to the lectures while I scramble over ancient walls and dart down hidden alleyways in search of special photo images. "Where's your husband?" the nervous tour guide invariably asks her. "Oh, don't worry," she dutifully replies. "He's nearby taking pictures and will return in time for our departure."

**Escapists:** Life can be Hell, filled with stress at work and the pressures of everyday living. Worse yet, life can become routine, filled with mundane and predictable events. For escapists, the antidote to this quagmire is to grab tennis racquets, golf clubs, snorkels, and swim fins and flee to beaches, resorts, golf courses, and tennis courts around the world. Once there, they put life's ups and downs behind them for a brief period of time. These are called get-away trips, and they often last for only a few days or a week tops. Some people travel this way their entire lives.

**Sun Worshippers:** This is an extreme variation of the escapist. Lying on beaches and around swimming pools all day and wining and dining at night are the highlights of their travel experiences. Dark suntans are essential when returning to the office; they are worn like badges of courage until they slowly fade away. Cruise ship enthusiasts are found in this group. They sun themselves on deck and eat about eight meals a day while cruising to places like the Caribbean. It's like floating around the world on Hawaii. Someone even asked me one time what I thought about taking a cruise in Hawaii. I said I thought it was redundant, which elicited a quizzical stare.

**Adventurers:** This is where those Australians fit in. There are two kinds of adventurers: those seeking serious physical conquests and those seeking soft adventure. Serious adventurers spend two weeks climbing to Mt. Everest's base camp, trekking across the Sahara desert, skiing in the Andes, bicycling across China, or riding a camel across the Australian outback. Not my cup of tea.

I prefer an adventure where I can get a hot shower and enjoy a glass of wine with a good meal at the end of the day. This is what I call soft adventure. Here's a good example: riding ponies before dawn to the Bromo Volcano in Indonesia. On that occasion, we rose in the middle of the night and departed by car from the quaint town of Tretes on the island of Java. It seemed like an ungodly hour to get up, but it was just as well. Had we stayed in bed, the local muezzin would have awakened us anyway when he called the local Muslims to prayer over the loudspeakers attached to his nearby mosque.

We drove through dark villages to a staging area for breakfast, then climbed on ponies for a magical ride into the black night. Our route took us across the floor of an ancient volcanic crater. As our ponies' hooves clopped over timeworn lava beds, we braced our feet in the stirrups and stared at the galaxies of stars floating like giant chandeliers above our heads. Each pony was led by a guide who trotted along beside us for our thirty minute trek. It was still dark when we dismounted and climbed a footpath to the rim of the brooding Bromo Volcano. We arrived just in time to watch dawn chase away the stars and transform the oily-black night into a fuzzy peach sunrise. Blue-grey mists hung over the lunar landscape below us, while the volcano vented sulfurous steam that smelled like eggs left in a compost bin. Silence engulfed us, a silence so vast, it wasn't hard to imagine one was standing on the moon. At last, the sun freed itself from the surrounding mountains and showered us in glorious pixels of orange, red, and golden light. It was with great reluctance that we eventually abandoned our princely realm and remounted our ponies, for it meant returning to the busy world of cars, airplanes, and loudspeakers calling Muslims to prayer.

I'm sure we could all come up with another category or two of world travelers, but you get the idea. Where do we all fit in? Who cares? As long as we enjoy ourselves, one thing is certain, the more we travel, the more likely we are to experience a few of those "memorable moments" when things spin out of control. Those moments can be quite stressful at the time, but they always make great stories later. It's an unwritten rule of travel that the more painful the event, the funnier it seems in retrospect. So, let's continue our journey around the world and see just how much trouble we can find.

# CHAPTER TWO
*Up, Up, and Away?*

Imagine you're sitting on the runway in an airplane with no pilots. This is confirmed by an automated cabin message that announces you are about to take part in a historic event: the first completely automated commercial airplane flight. The message drones on, pointing out what you already know. There is no pilot or co-pilot onboard. "But you need not worry," the melodic voice soothes, "because absolutely nothing can go wrong . . . go wrong . . . go wrong . . . go wrong . . .

Panic anyone? Okay, air travel isn't normally going to be that exciting, but as I noted in the first chapter, sometimes it has the potential to get a little more venturesome than we want. If you're lucky, the one thing that will *not* be memorable is your airline travel, but international travel nearly always begins with a flight to somewhere. Do that sort of thing often enough, and you're bound to run into some headwinds.

Anywhere you flew in the old Soviet Union was an adventure.

I have already shared the incident in Tbilisi, but there were a few other memorable moments. Fe and I were traveling on an independent itinerary, not in a group. That meant our flights generally left in the middle of the night. Tour groups got the daytime departures. We would arrive at the airport while it was still dark and be met by an official from Intourist, Russia's official travel agency. After checking in, the official would take us to our plane which was sitting on the tarmac. The passenger staircase was already in position, and light from the plane's interior revealed dozens of Uzbekistani, Georgians, or Russians milling about at the bottom of the stairs. No one was allowed to board before the pilots, so everyone stood around, waiting. That wasn't the worst of it, however. Once the pilots had ascended the stairs, all foreign travelers boarded next, a fact our Intourist guide impressed upon the hapless crowd when she began shoving people aside with all the charm of a KGB agent. (Would KGB agents have boarded before us, I wondered?) Fe and I quietly followed our version of Ivan the Terrible through the now restless crowd, our eyes cast on the pavement ahead of us, and climbed the stairs alone. Once we were seated, the flood gates opened and the frustrated throng charged up the stairs and into the bowels of the plane with all the grace of rioting spectators at a soccer match. Within minutes, every seat was filled. We never saw an empty seat on any of our flights.

In Samarkand, I made the mistake of taking the aisle seat in our assigned row, only to have that large Uzbek I mentioned in chapter one begin shouting at me. I couldn't understand a word he said, but no translation was needed. Clearly, he thought I was in his seat, although I was pretty sure my ticket gave me claim to it. I tried to stand my ground, or seat in this case, for fear that if I got up, I would have to stand all the way to our next destination. The man's six-foot-six frame, large, calloused hands, and scowling, unshaven face were very intimidating, and I wasn't sure what to do. Embarrassed, I glanced towards the stewardesses, but they seemed unfazed by the man's tirade and made no effort to clear up the confusion. Fe was seated by the window, and I noted that the middle seat remained empty. I suspected that was the seat where my Uzbek friend belonged, but when I finally gestured that I would move there, he seemed satisfied. Once I had shifted to my new, tighter quarters, he thumped down and proceeded to stuff his canvass bag full of melons into the tiny space between our legs. I averted my eyes from the man and began counting all the flies in the plane.

Our most embarrassing incident occurred when we landed in Bukhara, Uzbekistan. It was still dark, and rain was tumbling from the sky with the ferocity of wild beasts. To make matters worse, the pilot had parked his plane as far from the terminal as possible, even though the tarmac was nearly deserted. It seemed he wanted to test everyone's mettle. We saw no choice but to get as thoroughly drenched as the other passengers, many of whom were already running for the dimly lit sanctuary of the arrival lounge several hundred yards away. As we hurried down the stairs from the plane, however, we discovered an empty, double-coach bus just steps away with an Intourist guide holding an umbrella for us. What a glorious sight! The guide motioned for us to get inside, and we quickly hopped on board.

When the other passengers saw us, they immediately changed course and made a mad dash for our bus, but before they could join us, the Intourist guide held up her hand with all the authority of a New York traffic cop and shouted "nyet." (Nyet was the Russians' favorite word, by the way.) The poor people skidded to a halt and watched forlornly as the guide followed us onboard and closed the doors. It seemed the vast, empty bus was only for the two of us! Dozens of resigned gazes followed us as we were whisked away to the terminal.

We'll talk more about the weather in Chapter Four, but I bring it up now, because it can really wreck havoc with flight plans. One of the most awesome displays of nature's power I have ever witnessed occurred on the Amazon River in Brazil. I was standing by a river bank of a small tributary and admiring the changing light on the water's glassy surface when I heard the most amazing roar. It reverberated through the jungle's canopy with the ferocity of a pack of hungry tigers. The nearby trees shook as the roaring grew closer, but I knew it wasn't tigers because tigers don't run in packs and they don't climb trees. My next thought was army boots marching through the tree tops, but that didn't make any more sense than the tigers. At last it hit me. The roar was caused by approaching rain, and I was only seconds away from being inundated. I had never heard rain make so much noise in my life, and I set a personal best for the hundred yard dash, ducking under the cover of my lodge's bamboo roof just as the deluge swamped the ground where I'd been standing.

So how does this story relate to flying? I was on photo assignment in the Brazilian portion of the Amazon rain forest, and I was scheduled the next morning to fly in a single-engine plane downriver to a point where two separate tributaries of the Amazon River came together. It was called "the meeting of the waters," and what made it so interesting was the difference in coloration between the two systems. One side of the river was dirty brown while the other was as black as an evil knight. The black river was appropriately called the Rio Negro. Differences in water temperature, currents, and mineral content prevented the two rivers from mingling for several miles.

The pilot had thoughtfully removed the door on my side of the airplane so I could lean out and photograph straight down. Sound a bit crazy? I thought so. We took off from a small airport and headed down the river while I checked and rechecked my seat belt to make sure it was going to hold me.

The Amazon basin formed an amazing tapestry of images when seen from above. The lush, green rain forest spread beneath us like a rumpled carpet which was dissected here and there by ribbons of shiny, bruise-colored water. The river and its tributaries were so still, they reflected the sky's fluffy, white clouds and the radiant sun with the clarity of a giant mirror.

Did I mention clouds? As we approached our destination, a mountain of them suddenly boiled up the river towards us, but they weren't fluffy white. These were gray and black, and they towered menacingly over our heads. I immediately thought about

13

yesterday's cloud burst, and I knew this weather front meant business. So did my pilot. Without hesitation, he banked our tiny aircraft into a tight turn while he informed me that we would have to temporarily abort our mission. Then, he raced back up the river with the same sense of urgency I'd displayed the day before when I made my record setting dash to the safety of my lodge. The pilot didn't even bother trying to reach the smaller airport where we had taken off. He made a beeline for the international airport, which was closer, and landed the plane moments before the storm struck us.

It felt as though someone had playfully tipped over a gigantic bucket of water and dumped it on our heads while a giant fan blew hurricane force winds at us. Visibility was reduced to near zero; the tarmac became an instant lake; and the fierce winds tried their hardest to flip our little plane over on its back. My chest thumped with adrenalin at the thought of what might have happened if the pilot hadn't acted so swiftly.

Twenty minutes later, the storm had passed, and we took off once more. This time, I got my pictures, all the while keeping an uneasy look out for clouds that weren't fluffy white. I no longer worried about my seat belt.

We've all experienced long plane rides when we travel abroad, but on one trip to Asia, I thought I'd entered a time warp. Fe and I were on our way to Nepal, which required us to fly from San Francisco to Los Angeles to Seoul, South Korea, to Bangkok, Thailand, to Kathmandu, Nepal. We had made those kinds of trips before, so we were mentally and emotionally prepared for our quest. The first leg of our journey took us to Los Angeles where we arrived in plenty of time to catch our connecting, international flight. So far, so good. After a brief layover, we took off and resumed our journey. I settled contentedly into my seat and looked out the window in anticipation of seeing an endless expanse of blue-green ocean below me. Except there was no ocean; I was looking at land. I must admit that worried me a bit. I'd flown to Asia enough times to know that the only possible land sightings for many, many hours would be Catalina Island and Hawaii.

Disjointed thoughts spun through my head. Perhaps the pilot had forgotten something and was returning to the airport. Or he'd found a short cut. I shook my head to clear the cobwebs. I was being silly, and I knew it.

At last a smiling stewardess wandered down the aisle and I caught her attention. "Where are we going?" I asked. It was a stupid question, but she seemed to grasp my confusion and immediately set me straight. She told me that in order to catch the tail winds to Seoul, we had to fly up the coast to Vancouver. That meant retracing the route I had just taken that morning. In fact, as she explained this, the plane nearly flew over my house which I had left six hours ago. From the time Fe and I left home until we finally "hung a left" at the Canadian border, we had spent over nine hours traveling down the coast and back up again, and we hadn't even left the country yet! The airline needed a different name for that flight. Alice In Wonderland's Air Travel leapt to mind, but I supposed that name was protected by copyright.

As a travel photographer, I flew to some interesting places, including two trips to Tibet in the mid-1990s. I had always wanted to see Tibet and was delighted to have the opportunity. Actually, I didn't fly into Tibet the first time. Fe joined me on an overland journey from Kathmandu to Lhasa that was the adventure of a lifetime, but more about that later. The next year I returned alone to shoot some additional locations, and this time I planned to travel there by air. I anticipated a pretty normal trip, but things quickly spun out of control. When I arrived in Kathmandu, I learned that my land operator had not been able to secure a visa for me, and I spent the next three days trying to obtain one from the Chinese government.

There were three reasons why my visa was being denied: 1) China didn't like people entering Tibet alone . . . they wanted everybody in tour groups where they could keep an eye on them; 2) My first name happened to coincide with someone on their "do not let into Tibet" list, and the fact that my last name had nothing in common with the other's seemed of no consequence; and 3) A United States senator had recently visited Tibet and raised such a

15

public furor over China's continued occupation of the hapless country that the Chinese government was even more paranoid than usual about Americans going there.

So, I sat in Kathmandu while my land operator, Mr. Ma, pleaded with the Chinese consulate. I was about to give up and go home when my agent received a last minute approval. Mr. Ma told me that the consulate who stamped my passport declared, "This is the last independent visa I will issue into Tibet!"

The overland trip that I had taken with Fe the year before was a five day journey, but my flight from Kathmandu would get me to Lhasa in a matter of hours. That's what I was told, anyway. So there I was, visa in hand, floating along at 30,000 feet and scanning the landscape below for the pot-holed, dust-infested dirt road that my wife and I had traversed the year before. You might wonder how I could hope to see a dirt road from 30,000 feet. The answer is simple. Tibet ranges in altitude between 12,000 and 17,000 feet. I was flying a lot closer to the ground than normal.

Tibet was just as amazing to see from the air as the Amazon. The rumpled carpet analogy still applied, only now it was comprised of desolate valley floors ringed by the Himalayas and other dramatic mountain ranges. Rain rarely fell there, and the landscape was so bleak, it looked like an endless desert, forsaken and lost, that had been cast into the sky and abandoned. In reality, it was a mountain kingdom whose roots reached back into the murky depths of history.

Despite the arid climate, water was actually quite plentiful in Tibet, thanks to the many rivers flowing down from the surrounding glacial mountains. During our overland journey, we often turned a corner and came upon handfuls of flinty Tibetans using those icy water taps to grow barley and wheat during the brief, summer season.

I fondly recalled those scenes as I hurtled through the sky towards Lhasa, and I looked forward returning to a country where people turned prayer wheels to release goodwill into the world, yaks decorated with colorful ribbons were used to plow the fields, and the population's Buddhist faith was mixed with more ancient

Bon beliefs that gave credence to spirits in inanimate objects.

I was particularly pleased with myself for outlasting that official in Kathmandu and obtaining my precious visa. Life was good, and I was certain nothing could go wrong . . . go wrong . . . go wrong.

On our approach to Lhasa, however, my optimism began to waver. Clouds the size of small countries loomed ahead. As I watched, they thickened and transformed themselves into a formidable barrier. The pilot announced our descent without preamble, but I wasn't reassured. His monotone voice reminded me of the recording in my little witticism at the beginning of this chapter. Before long, we were buffeted by strong winds, and the plane bounced along in the thick clouds until I became so disoriented I couldn't be certain what direction we were traveling.

Across the aisle, a Tibetan man of indeterminate age was fingering a string of prayer beads in his hand. He'd pulled them from his pocket before takeoff and had been praying all the way to Lhasa. With each bump of our aircraft, his prayers grew more intense as his head bobbed in rhythm to his murmuring voice, and his fingers flew along the beads. That, I decided, was not a good sign. Time passed. How many minutes I couldn't be certain, but more than enough to land. My mood grew morbid as I stared out my window at the grey veil enveloping my world. Then I looked up and saw blue sky peeking in and out of the cumulus clouds surrounding the plane. Whatever the pilot was doing, one thing was certain. He wasn't landing. I was beginning the think that my return trip to Tibet was jinxed, that I would never see those Buddhist monks and prayer wheels again. Sure enough, the pilot's voice suddenly droned through the cabin to inform us that we couldn't land in Lhasa due to the heavy storm. The flight would continue to its next destination: Chengdu in the heart of China!

My fate was sealed. I was about to fly to the middle of the country that had occupied Tibet for nearly half a century. As I tried to cope with this new situation, my eyes were drawn to the Tibetan across the aisle, who was now praying harder than ever. How would it feel, I wondered, to learn you were going to land in the

17

middle of the country that invaded yours nearly fifty years ago? What fears were going through his mind? I tried to imagine landing in North Korea or some other hostile land. It was an unsettling sensation.

Unsettling sensations were to pursue me for rest of that day and night. There was no return flight to Tibet until the following morning, and I was told I would have to spend the night in Chengdu. Arrangements were being made for me at a nearby hotel. That was the least of my worries. The stewardesses on the flight spoke English, and they'd kept me informed of developments. The moment I stepped off the airplane, however, all recognizable communications ended. English was sucked into a giant black hole of Chinese voices. I was surrounded by a cacophony of words I couldn't begin to fathom, and no one understood me. It felt as though I'd been shipwrecked and thrown upon a distant shore. In a way, I supposed I had.

After being taken to a room where I could retrieve my luggage, I made my way through a maze of security and passport control procedures. That involved moving along in a crowd of jostling Chinese who were all determined to get through customs before me. Whether any of them were going to my hotel, I didn't know. Nor did I have a clue whether anyone would meet me once I entered the airport terminal. It did no good to ask those around me. They simply gave me blank stares and moved on.

Then a miracle happened. I heard someone talking in English! Much to my relief, I turned around and discovered an American tour guide behind me who was leading a small group of fellow Americans on a trip to Tibet. He spoke fluent Chinese and after a spirited discussion with the immigration official, he assured me that we would all be transported to the same hotel for the night. I nearly hugged the poor man, and tagged along after him like a lost puppy.

Sure enough, once we were finished with the immigration procedures we were herded outside to a waiting bus that whisked us off to a nearby building that looked more like a hostel than a hotel, but I didn't care. I was exhausted from my ordeal and looked forward to escaping to the solitude of my room. Only one small hurdle remained. The tour guide informed me during check-in that I would have to pay extra for a private room, even though all my pre-paid arrangements had included that little luxury. Nor would they accept U.S. currency. Luckily, I was able to exchange dollars for yuan with the guide, and I paid the extra fee for the private room without complaint. To whom would I have complained even if I wanted to, and in what language?

The hotel's interior was the equivalent of a Motel Six without an elevator, so I hoisted my luggage and climbed the stairs to the third floor, where I encountered a young woman in a gray uniform standing behind a small counter. Each floor was guarded by one of these women, and mine began chattering at me in a steady stream of Chinese while she walked me down a thinly carpeted hallway and opened the door to my room. I gestured that I couldn't understand a thing she said, but that didn't discourage her. She kept talking while I hauled my luggage into an almost barren room with one small throw rug in the middle of the floor, and no wall paintings or television.

The lack of décor caused my escort's voice to echo off the walls and floor in a most disconcerting way. I still had no idea why she was so excited, but I decided that ignorance was bliss. Best, I thought, to ignore her and hope she would go away. She stood in the doorway eyeing me. I smiled, she smiled back, and I closed the door. There was a moment of hesitation and silence, followed by the brisk sound of footsteps retreating along the thin carpet.

The accommodations were actually better than I expected. There was a big bed, a small writing desk, and a bathroom that could have fit into my closet back home. It did have a shower, however, and when I checked, hot water. The travel gods were smiling on me. I could overlook a lot of things after a hot shower.

Dinner consisted of a prepared group meal for all the plane's passengers in the main dining hall. The American tour group occupied a large, round table in the far corner, and I recognized a few faces at other, smaller tables. There was no sign of the Tibetan with the prayer beads, however.

I had to admit that the food was both tasty and hearty. It restored my sense of well-being and adventure to the point that I decided to stroll a bit before dark. The American guide had told me on the way to the hotel that Chengdu was the gateway to some very scenic mountains, and I assumed the local population was used to foreigners. Such was not the case. I was the only Caucasian in sight, and I felt dozens of eyes following me everywhere I went. I looked in shop windows and watched young adults and families playing board games along the sidewalks. There was even a video shop, but I saw no signs of Harrison Ford or Meryl Streep on the store's posters.

Many couples and friends strolled the streets chatting and laughing together. I had no doubt that at least some of those conversations were about me, but everyone seemed content and I felt quite safe.

I returned to my hotel ready for a good night's rest, figuring I would need my energy for tomorrow's return to Tibet, but I sensed immediately that all was not right. My Chinese floor attendant was waiting for me with a piece of paper in hand and her mouth going a-mile-a-minute. This time, she followed me into my room and continued talking as rapidly as possible, as if the sheer volume of her words would overcome our language barrier. She pointed behind me, and it was then that I noticed a rug rolled up in a corner of the room. Was she trying to sell me a souvenir, I wondered? Upon closer inspection, I saw clothing tucked inside the carpet, and I realized to my dismay that it was somebody's belongings. At last, I understood my young companion's verbal assault. She was telling me that I was to have a roommate for the night.

I didn't exactly panic, but I could feel a hot rush of adrenalin shooting through my veins. I'm a light sleeper, and images of a snoring, toilet-flushing companion were not comforting. Not to mention the fact that we would have to share the bed! That would not do, I thought. I'd paid for a private room not once but twice. Firm action was needed. I waved my hands and shook my head emphatically, then picked up the homemade luggage, carried it into the hallway, and plunked it down. My act of rebellion was accomplished over the loud protests of my attendant, who followed me waving her piece of paper. She had barely cleared the doorway when I jumped back into my room and closed the door. There was no latch or inside lock, so I hastily grabbed the wooden chair by the writing desk and shoved it against the door knob, just like in the movies. I looked around for something to reinforce my feeble barrier, but there was nothing else unless I wanted to shove the writing desk across the room. Heart thrumming, I put my ear to the door and listened. Silence greeted me, although I could have sworn that I heard the young woman breathing out there in the hallway. I could also have sworn she was breathing in Chinese. At least, she was no longer talking, which I took as a good sign. But there was no sound of retreating footsteps, and that worried me. At any moment, I expected an assault on my door, but when nothing happened, I finally gave up, got undressed, jumped into bed, and pulled the pillow over my head. I waited and listened for the sound of my chair being scraped across the wooden floor as the door was forced open, but all remained quiet. Fatigue eventually overpowered me, and I slept. When I awoke the next morning, I was relieved to see that the other half of my bed was still empty.

Breakfast and check-out couldn't happen quickly enough for me. I followed the American tour group back on the bus and returned to the airport, where we all boarded a domestic flight to Lhasa. I was pleased to see my Tibetan neighbor across the aisle, although he looked like he'd spent a sleepless night.

I was equally pleased to see that the weather was now brilliantly clear, and we landed in Tibet without further ado. It appeared that my jinx had departed with my unwanted roommate's luggage.

# CHAPTER THREE
*Breathing in Another Language*

In the first chapter, I mentioned that some people travel to escape from the stress of their daily lives. They take get-away trips and often end up luxuriating on a golden beach or sporting in an exotic resort in some remote part of the world. Think Bora Bora, an island a lot like Kauai, except the locals speak French and have French bread delivered to their mailboxes. Or Bali, Indonesia, where I was told the native women still wore sarongs around their waist and little else. That turned out to be true, but only among the older women who had done so all their lives. The younger women dressed more modestly.

Such flights-of-fancy take travelers away from their everyday surroundings. Enjoyment is derived from momentarily giving oneself up to some hedonistic pleasure. Heck, we all need an escape plan once in awhile.

For others, travel is more of a pilgrimage, a quest to gain new insights into others and themselves through personal experiences.

As a "soft adventurer," I fall into this latter group. We quest-seekers enjoy immersing ourselves in new cultures and visiting unusual places we've never seen before. Our goal is to discover adventures beyond the realm of everyday life. The spirit of the destination becomes the motivation for the journey.

World travel is both exhilarating and personal. Each of us seeks something unique from the undertaking, something that adds to our self-perception and understanding of other ways of life. If our purpose is the quest rather than the escape, it's not sufficient to merely visit a country. We must be willing to immerse ourselves in its unique customs and explore places that are more off the beaten track.

Here's an example of what I'm talking about. Not too long ago, Fe and I joined a group to Morocco. In Marrakech, the tour guide took us to visit the famous medina in the early afternoon. In the main square, called Jamaa el Fna, there were a few entertainers and merchants selling souvenirs, but the air was hot and the mood sleepy. That night, most of our group chose to eat at a restaurant, but a few of us took taxis and returned to the square. What a transformation! People who have been there at night use phrases like "assault on the senses," "going back in time," and "absolute mayhem" to describe their experiences. The medina and Jamaa el Fna were all of that and more. Every inch of the square was contested by snake charmers, wrestlers, t-shirt vendors throwing samples into the crowds, henna tattoo artists, performing monkeys, street entertainers, and stalls filled with oranges, snails, and various kinds of nuts. Best of all, tiny food stalls had magically sprouted around the square. The stalls consisted of low counters with chairs surrounding a small cook stove. Young men behind the counters pushed menus at customers and spoke rapidly in broken English. Fe and I took seats at one of the counters and chose food items at random. The food was hot and quite tasty. The night air was charged with the frenzied voices of waiters calling to customers and vendors hawking their wares. It was a carnival atmosphere that spiced our food and stimulated our senses.

When we had finished our meal, our waiter brought our bill,

which was very reasonable, and I pulled out my dirham to pay him. He claimed he didn't have the right change, so he took my dirham to another food vendor and brought back smaller bills, which he returned, minus the amount for our dinners. At that point, he began to shout "teep, teep, teep" which I understood to mean tip. I was perfectly happy to include a "teep," but first there was the matter of the money he'd given me. It wasn't enough. He'd short changed me. It was only a few dirham, but I wasn't about to let the man con me. I showed him his mistake, but he waved his hand and said "no, no, no," the change was correct. I showed him his error a second time, but he continued to deny it and asked for a "teep," once more. I finally looked him in the eye, pointed at the money in his hand, and said: "Guess what. The money you shorted me *is* your "teep." With that, Fe and I got up to leave. The waiter quickly realized that he had just short changed himself (he would have gained more from a reasonable tip) and tried to make amends, but it was too late. I smiled as we left, not certain which had been more fun: eating at the food stall in the square, or matching wits with the waiter over the change and his "teep."

World travel requires an open mind and a commitment to learning. It challenges us to filter our new experiences through our personal value systems in a way that helps us appreciate the differences between our world and others. That is what makes foreign travel so special, and when we are successful, the resulting cultural exchanges, historical perspectives, and unique images leave lasting impressions. These are the things we carry back with us to our more familiar surroundings. They are more than just photographs or memories, for they have become woven into the fabric of our lives.

It's like learning to breathe in another language. To really learn a foreign language, it's not enough to simply translate popular phrases. We must learn how to emphasize certain words, how to roll the tongue, and when to inhale or exhale. Only then can we hope to form the words properly. It's the same with travel. It's not enough to "fart and go," as my sister-in-law says. We must look beyond the standard tourist fare to feel the pulse and heartbeat of the land and its people.

This book is filled with places and experiences that have helped Fe and myself learn to breathe in new, unexpected ways. Sometimes, it's not so much the adventure as the destination itself that stands out. Here are a few places that had an uncommon effect on us. They are places that, in some small way, have altered our perspective on life just by being there.

### CHINA'S GREAT WALL IN WINTER

Snow obscured my view as my driver slowed the car on an icy curve. The road normally used to reach the Great Wall was closed due to winter storms, but my guide had suggested we try an alternate route to a new section of the wall that had recently been opened. We were close, he told me, but the wall was not yet visible through the white haze of snowflakes tumbling from an endless expanse of clouds that hung like sodden laundry over the winter landscape. And the driver was in no hurry. Not on that slick road.

My mind whirled through mental snapshots of large crowds crawling in ant-like fashion along the Wall, and nearby vendors hawking postcards and souvenirs. Those were typical summer scenes when thousands of people visited the Wall each day. It didn't seem likely that I would have to worry about such crowds now. I had arrived in Beijing in January. Not the best time of year to go sightseeing, but there I was. Snow covered everything. Soft, fluffy snow that reminded me of fields of rabbits' pelts. Trees stretched their skeletal branches across a bleak sky. Local people bundled themselves in old, blue-grey Mao jackets to protect them from the cold. And it *was* cold! Still, my hosts wanted me to see their important landmarks, including the Great Wall.

Not that I was complaining. The Great Wall had always been on my "must visit" list, and the prospect of finally seeing it sent fireworks of anticipation bursting through me. This was a structure that had first been built in the 7th century B.C. It was originally designed to protect independent warring states from one another. Later, it protected a unified China from Mongols and other invaders. Astronauts could even see it from space as it snaked in serpentine fashion four thousand miles across China's verdant, rolling hillsides. To them, it must have looked like a giant reptile in search of its next meal.

At last, we approached a small parking area near the base of a rocky hill, and I got my first look at the wall. It loomed above me in the snowy light like a timeless frigate riding atop a rocky wave. The popular section of the wall visited in the summer required visitors to ascend only a few steps to its ramparts. Not so here. I was going to have to climb a steep stairway the equivalent of three football stadiums to the cheap seats.

Or not. Two guides with donkeys were waiting for me, and each offered to carry me to the top for a small fee. I had to admit the idea was appealing, but riding a donkey up to the Great Wall clashed with my sense of adventure. The Wall was something to be conquered, not served up on the back of a furry animal. I waved them off with a polite shake of my head, and began the steep ascent on foot.

As I neared the halfway point, my legs were beginning to tire and my breathing was coming in more frequent puffs. My thoughts drifted to the two donkeys I had so cavalierly dismissed at the bottom of the hill. Maybe, riding to the top hadn't been such a bad idea after all. Can you guess who was waiting for me around the next turn? Of course you can -- those same, eager guides with their donkeys. How tempting those beasts of burden looked to me now! I flirted with the idea of asking how much they charged for the remainder of the journey, if for no other reason than to confirm my suspicion that their rates had probably risen, now that I was tiring and out of breath. After a brief inner struggle, I resolved not to give up. I smiled at the men's enterprise but resisted their urgent entreaties. I'd be darned if I was going to quit now. I kept climbing.

When the top finally hove into view, I knew I had made the right decision. Rarely have I been so rewarded for my perseverance as I was that day. I stepped onto the Wall's ramparts and was greeted by a deep, unfathomable silence. It was a top-of-the-world kind of silence. A silence that stretched back for centuries. Nothing moved in the falling snow. I was peering through a lace curtain of fluffy snowflakes at a world without a trace of mankind. Not one footprint could be found. Not one figure was visible.

The air was as crisp as freshly harvested lettuce, and I inhaled several deep breaths to clear my mind. This must be what it's like to summit a famous mountain, I thought. The Great Wall had become my Everest, and while my conquest was small, the exhilaration was just as real. In both directions the abandoned Wall undulated away from my vantage point across a landscape of ghostly foothills. Close up, its roughhewn, stone features stood in sharp contrast to the snow, but in the distance the ramparts blended with the gauzy hills and valleys until details grew vague, then disappeared altogether.

Below me, a guard station had been built into the wall. Centuries ago it would have housed soldiers armed with swords and bows and arrows. Theirs must have been a lonely vigil, their days filled with boredom and tedium . . . until the enemy appeared. Imagine what it must have felt like to suddenly see marauding bands of Mongolian invaders swarming through the valleys towards the wall. Warnings would have sounded, alerting soldiers who hastily raced to the parapets and fit arrows to bows in anticipation of battle. Messengers from the guard house would have been dispatched requesting reinforcements.

The longer I stood there, the more time bent away from me. I could *hear* the thundering hooves of the intruders' horses, the heavy breathing of both rider and animal, and the bloodthirsty cries of would-be conquerors seeking pillage and glory; I could *feel* their consternation when they reined in their horses before those massive walls. What would have been their reaction, I wondered, when presented with such an impenetrable barrier? Bewilderment, surely . . . followed by frustration . . . then anger. Stomping horses churning the snow beneath their feet, defiant voices echoing off the massive wall, and raised weapons shaking in broad-knuckled fists would have had no effect.

The leaders most likely gathered beyond the range of the

defenders' arrows to discuss options and plot strategies. War parties would have ventured forth to inspect the wall for weaknesses that could be breached. When nothing presented itself, scouts were likely sent off to search for less protected ramparts or a way around the wall. How many days would they have ridden before they returned with the discouraging news that the wall stretched into eternity? How long would it take for the marauders' leaders to realize their only option was to turn around and ride away, defeated?

TIBET

Somewhere high above the plains and valleys of the known world stood an ancient civilization that had remained hidden for centuries behind a massive fortress of mountain ranges. It floated beyond the grasp of early adventurers and explorers like a cloud drifting in space. Stories and rumors abounded from Asian traders who had been there, but there was little evidence to show the Western world that such a place existed at all, except in the minds of a few intrepid travelers. Enshrouded in mystery, this far-away land seemed more a state of mind than reality.

Until the early 1900s, no westerner had reached Tibet's holy city, Lhasa, and little light from the outside world had penetrated the country's icy realms. Entering the country meant facing challenges and hardships only a handful of adventurers were willing to endure. If they entered from India or Nepal, they had to climb the Himalayas, and from China, they faced equally formidable mountain ranges. Once they'd conquered those obstacles, they had to trek through valleys bristling with unknown dangers, including robbers and thieves who lurked along their route. Mountain passes as high as 17,000 feet had to be crossed, often in the face of fierce blizzards. Landslides and avalanches added to their perils. In case of illness, herbs were the only medicines available, and medical treatment often consisted of rituals performed by a local shaman.

Yet the most formidable barrier was the Tibetans themselves. They did not want their realm disturbed; westerners were not allowed in their country. When intruders were discovered, the Tibetans threw them out. It took a British army to finally reach Lhasa in 1905, and they did it by force. Britain feared Russia was gaining too much influence over possible trade and military routes, but when Colonel Younghusband finally led his troops into the holy city, all he found was an ancient culture that had little interest in the outside world. The army left, and the country closed its borders, again.

A photo assignment gave me the chance to follow in the footsteps of these intrepid adventurers when Fe and I traveled overland from Kathmandu to Lhasa. Our journey wasn't as heroic as theirs, but we encountered our own hazards and experienced the excitement of their quest. We set forth with a small group in a van about the size of an old VW bus, and we soon found ourselves negotiating the same tortuous Himalayan mountain passes taken by those who came before us. Our route consisted of an uncharitably narrow road cut into the sheer granite walls that surrounded us. The road was better suited for donkeys than vehicles, but it was the only way in or out of Tibet.

As the wheels of the van danced within a few feet of the precipice, I looked down at giant boulders that had tumbled into the river bed far below. The boulders served as a stark reminder of the violence that regularly visited these mountain passes. They warned us not to take our safety for granted, a warning that was quickly reinforced when we arrived at a stone bridge that had been so badly battered by rock slides, it was no longer considered safe for a van filled with passengers. Our guide feared the bridge could no longer bear the weight of both us and the vehicle, so we abandoned it and hurried across the rickety span on foot, then watched anxiously as our van followed.

We even drove through a glacier on a narrow road cut through the living ice, but none of these adventures prepared me for the vast plateau that embodies Tibet. Stretching before me was a barren landscape of windswept valleys where little grew except hardscrabble, and winter hovered just a few hundred feet above my head. The world I knew had vanished, and my minivan became a time capsule that carried me back through centuries of praying monks, dangerous spirits, and spinning prayer wheels. The narrow, dust-choked, dirt road followed by the van became the only reference point to life as I knew it. I was wandering on the rooftop of the world, floating somewhere between the earth and the sky.

OURO PRETO, BRAZIL

Sunrise is a special time for a photographer. Lighting is as sharp as a warrior's sword, and subjects stand out in sharp relief from their surroundings. It's also a time of peaceful solitude. Tourists are still asleep, and few residents have ventured forth. The world momentarily becomes a still life frozen between night and day. It's a perfect time to explore back streets and discover hidden passageways.

Such were my mornings in Ouro Preto, a Portuguese village that had changed little from its colonial days. At dawn, mists bathed the cobblestone streets and gently sloping valleys in radiant, blue undertones. Other than an occasional solitary figure hurrying along one of the steep walkways, his footsteps clipping the stone sidewalk with a tok-tok-tok sound that echoed among the surrounding buildings, the streets were empty. Street lamps cast a yellow glow on rows of whitewashed houses, whose moss-colored, tile roofs sloped gently into the valleys below. Frilly clouds partially obscured a full moon that crept towards a range of rolling foothills beyond the town. Remnants of night's dark shadows struggled in vain to hide but couldn't escape from the rapidly expanding morning light.

Tucked away among the low-lying hills of central Brazil, Ouro Preto was a beautifully preserved nineteenth-century village. Its' colloquial charm cried out for even the most jaded traveler to stop and stay awhile. Donkeys loaded with firewood waited patiently along narrow lanes for their masters; a gypsy's child bathed in water streaming from the mouths of gargoyles in a public drinking fountain; rays of sunlight highlighted the ornate towers and crosses of the thirteen baroque churches for which the village was famous. UNESCO had declared Ouro Preto a world treasure, and it was easy to see why.

Treasure was certainly one reason to go there. Originally made famous for its black gold, which accounted for the town's name, Ouro Preto was also renowned for some of the world's finest gemstones and jewelry, including the rare Imperial Topaz, a light-colored, golden-yellow stone that often shaded to a pink cast. It was no longer mined anywhere else in the world.

The town's spirit was captured for me in the modern paintings of Carlos Bracher, an artist whose simple studio overlooked the town from the back of his home. When Fe and I visited him, we discovered a vibrant man in his fifties who expressed as much passion for his town as he did for his art. Together, we strolled along the streets and shared our delight in the artistic visions created by late-afternoon sunlight – Carlos, through the power of his artistic eye and I, through the lens of my camera. Those images included tree branches backlit against a pale-white wall, the dome of a baroque church turned to a mustard color by the warmth of the sun, the bend in a shiny, cobblestone street, and a row of whitewashed shops trimmed in deep browns and rust reds.

We ended our explorations in the main square of Praca Tiradentas where students from the local university were acting out dramas and dancing across the uneven stones in flowing costumes and garish masks. There, Fe and I said goodbye to our new friend and watched him slip away among the throng of costumed youths.

In an odd sort of way, Ouro Preto reminded me of Tibet. Both possessed a timeless quality that seemed to turn minutes into days and days into centuries. Looking back, I can still see the smiling face of Bracher disappearing into the crowd, but I no longer know if he was real or a dream stretched through the prism of time.

VENICE, ITALY

Talk about lighting! Imagine yourself standing on the Ponte della Paglia footbridge looking at the Bridge of Sighs, a covered bridge that spans the narrow canal dividing the Doge's Palace from its dreaded dungeons. It's said that when prisoners crossed the bridge on their way to face the judgment of their inquisitors, they

31

looked out the bridge's tiny windows and sighed, because they knew they would never see Venice again.

And thus its name.

I'm the one sighing now, but for a different reason. Millions of people have stood where I stand and stared at the bridge, but only a handful have stood there at dawn, as I do now. The canal's dark water is calm. No gondola or motorboat has yet stirred its surface. The only hint of movement comes from a light breeze that gives the water a glazed look, much like the surface of a dark-green, candied apple.

Further down the canal, electric lights cast a spectrum of colorful reflections on the water. They remind me of the Northern lights in Alaska. As I watch, the first rays of morning sunlight suddenly strike the tall windows of the Palace to my left. The windows redirect the light back across the narrow canal onto the walls of the prison to my right, creating mottled patterns of warmth on the cool stones. The effect does not last long, but for a few brief moments, the canal has been transformed into a symphony of sparkling reflections and brilliant hues.

There I go again, extolling the virtues of getting up at dawn, but that is the best time to fully appreciate Venice . . . when the first fingers of morning light slip along the Grand Canal with the stealth of cats' paws. Venice is nearly void of people at that hour and filled with magic. In the Piazza San Marcos, neat rows of yellow chairs rest in front of shuttered cafes. Just a few hours ago throngs of tourists sat in those chairs sipping wine and listening to chamber music dancing on the evening air. Now, the Piazza is cemetery silent. The hordes of pigeons that frequent the square by day have yet to stir from their roosts around St. Mark's Basilica. Walk under the colonnades and all you will hear is the echo of your own footsteps.

The morning's sleepy mood quickly changes when sunlight startles the landscape and brings it to life. The street lamps blink off without warning. Tiled rooftops suddenly glimmer in the early sunlight. The cool white marble of the Santa Maria Della Salute Church blushes pink. New details quickly emerge. A small pool of water from an earlier shower flickers in the reflective glow of the emerging light. Rain drops shimmer like diamonds on the red, vinyl table tops of the outdoor cafes near the Rialto Bridge. A chorus line of barbershop-style poles rise from the water in front of fifteenth, sixteenth and seventeenth century Gothic, Renaissance and Byzantine palaces.

Venice is a time machine that flawlessly blends its brilliant past with the twenty-first century, and just when it seems like time has been frozen forever, the city stirs. A vaporetto roils the calm waters as it makes its first trip up the Grand Canal. Food vendors arrive with boatloads of vegetables, fruits and meats for the marketplace. A handful of lonely figures hurry along the narrow streets. There are no signs of tourists yet, but it is only a matter of time. Soon the quiet squares and canals will echo with the sounds of motorboats and vaporettos churning along the canals and the busy-bee buzz of tourists' voices as people get their first look at the Bridge of Sighs.

HONG KONG

A tired freighter wearily dropped its anchor in the harbor and was immediately surrounded by junks jostling one another for a favorable position to unload the ship's cargo. But one junk, a wooden boat with two, rust-colored sails splayed like twin fans up their respective masts, ignored the bedlam. It crossed the bay, instead, with the steady drum beat of a long-distance runner. I tried to imagine its destination. China, perhaps? That was still a land of mystery I would not be able to visit during my first trip to Hong Kong. It was only a few heartbeats away yet far removed from my world. Few westerners had seen China since Mao Tse-Tung's Communist Revolution took control of the country.

The year was 1969, and I had just arrived in the British Crown Colony of Hong Kong, also known as the "fragrant harbor." It was a magical place back then, one filled with mysteries that ignited one's imagination. Perhaps my view was a bit too romanticized, but I couldn't help being entranced by the enigmatic nature of the place. Every time I thought about my exotic destination, shivers of expectation raced up and down my spine. I had visions of opium dens, smugglers, and Communist spies lurked behind the glistening buildings standing before me.

It would be hard for modern travelers to understand why my imagination was running wild, but the Hong Kong I first visited was a very different place than it is today. Victoria Island was an enclave of English residences where British officers and civilians lived in the grand style of colonial rulers. Aberdeen Bay, on the back side of the island, was a quaint fishing village filled with so many wooden boats that one could walk from deck-to-deck across the bay without ever touching the water. It was possible for fishermen to live their entire lives without ever setting foot on land, their needs fulfilled by floating food merchants and other vendors. Today, Victoria Island is a forest of modern high-rise office buildings, and most of the boats have been relocated to places far removed from Aberdeen Bay.

China had not yet opened its doors to the outside world back then, so in order to catch a glimpse of it, I rode a crowded, steamy bus through the New Territories past verdant landscapes of flooded rice paddies, flocks of ducks, and ponds filled with algae to the Lok Ma Chau lookout point. From there, I could gaze across a meandering river at the mysterious country. I had been told that Hong Kong's fate was closely intertwined with China's. The British colony was China's eyes and ears to the outside world, and a great deal of illicit trade ran through Hong Kong's ports. Money to and from China secretly snaked its way through Hong Kong's banks. China needed Hong Kong, which was one reason it had not attempted to take the country away from the British by force.

As I stared across the divide that separated China from its brethren, a heavily-laden junk under full sail floated down the river, and I thought about the junk I had seen in Hong Kong harbor. Could it be the same one now returning to Hong Kong, its hold filled with illegal Chinese goods? Smugglers regularly plied those waters, so I knew anything was possible.

Today, the smugglers are gone, and the New Territories are defined by cities of towering apartment buildings and modern roads. The algae ponds and ducks have disappeared, replaced by forests of tenements and miles of concrete.

## PETRA

Petra is the Greek word for stone, a fitting name for a city that was literally carved from cliffs of soft, red rock. Two thousand years ago, Petra was a major trading center in what is now Jordan, but it was abandoned by the Nabataeans, who built it, and claimed by fierce Bedouins who guarded the place from unwanted intruders.

Petra is also known as the "forgotten city," because it disappeared from world view for centuries, remaining hidden behind a wall of mountains until 1812 when a Swiss explorer rediscovered it. It was no easy task for him. If the Bedouins had known he was a westerner and a Christian, they would have most likely killed him on the spot. He fooled them by learning Arabic and posing as a Persian pilgrim. It was a dangerous undertaking, but his reward was handsome, for he cast the light of the outside world on one of the more amazing cities of ancient times.

My entrance to Petra was not so dramatic, but I must admit I felt the rare chill of discovery as I entered the mountain range that had hidden the city for something in the neighborhood of seven centuries. I followed a narrow cleft, called the siq, which wound for over half-a-mile among sheer, canyon walls that soared hundreds of feet above my head. The effect was both exhilarating and claustrophobic. People hurried past, eager to reach the other end of the siq, but I wandered and lingered along the route. Remnants of caves, some with stone steps leading up to them, and strange wall markings peppered my route. There was something almost spiritual about the place, and I wanted to feel the full force of its magic.

At last, the narrow gap widened to reveal a colossal building, called the Treasury, which was carved out of the solid rock. This was what people were in such a hurry to see. It became famous in 1989 thanks to the movie Indiana Jones and the Last Crusade which staged the final, climactic scenes there. No movie could prepare me for the moment I first saw it, however; I stood there in awe. Sunlight cast the façade's giant columns into sharp relief from the decorative roof lines and sculpted porticoes. The building was so large, it seemed better suited for giants than for mortal men, and its location in the narrow confines of the siq only added to its prominence. No one seems to know why it was called the treasury. Scholars believe it was more likely a tomb, of which there are many in Petra, but I didn't care. Standing there made me feel as though I had found the holy grail, just like Indiana Jones did in the movie.

From there, a brief walk through a wider siq brought me to a valley pockmarked with caves and tombs, all carved into the face of the rock. Many of the cliffs were grooved with intricate patterns of striated blue, red, and ochre hues, as if artists had used the rock walls for their canvasses. There were so many things to see, including the ruins of the Great Temple and an amphitheatre. It would take many pages to elaborate on all of them, but there is one other building that merits special attention: the Monastery. To reach it, I had to walk over a mile through the valley and climb ancient stairways of roughhewn stones high into a mountain beyond the valley floor. The trail switched back and forth up dozens of steep, narrow canyons before reaching the top.

It took the better part of an hour to reach my goal, and the ascent was a lot more demanding than the climb to the Great Wall in winter. Those who didn't want to make the climb could rent donkeys and ride to the top, but like the Wall, the physical climb was far more satisfying. After one last push through a narrow chasm, with leg muscles burning and breaths coming in short, hot bursts, I emerged onto a plateau and stood before the Monastery. What a magnificent structure it was! Carved out of a rocky outcrop, its architecture and size were similar to the Treasury's, and like the former building, this one seemed to flow from the rock in a cascading series of columns and porticoes. But the Monastery was not wedged into a narrow siq; it stood in an airy, open square that let me stand back and enjoy a much broader perspective. The Treasury had towered over me like an ancient, high-rise, office building, but the Monastery appeared more like a throne surrounded by its protective cape of rocks.

## THE DEAD SEA

I have never been able to float on my back. I'm too thin for one thing, and I don't seem to have the knack for it. That changed when I got to the Dead Sea. Because there is no outlet for the water, its only escape is through evaporation, which causes minerals, particularly salt, to slowly accumulate. The sea is now so salty, it's impossible to swim or sink in it. You just fall onto your back and float! What a delightful experience. At last, I could lie on a water bed without the mattress and stare up at the cloudless sky. I know this doesn't rate on the scale of Petra or those other destinations I have covered, but sometimes life is about simpler pleasures.

# CHAPTER FOUR
*The Sun Never Shines In Prague*

I was standing just inside the doorway of a restaurant in Anchorage, Alaska, looking at the Anchorage Westward Hotel across the street and trying to decide what to do. It was January, and although I was bundled into the kind of sweater, gloves, and fur-lined overcoat that would keep me warm under normal circumstances, the current weather was anything but normal. Hurricane force winds were howling down the street at 80+ miles per hour, and the chill factor was so low (-40 degrees), the rooms on the windward side of my hotel couldn't hold heat. The main lobby and lounge area had morphed into a refugee camp for those who couldn't keep warm in their rooms. Fortunately, my room was on the leeward side of the building where it was chilly, but livable.

None of which helped my current dilemma . . . how to get back across the street to my hotel. I had ventured across the icy street before the wind had reached its current level of intensity, but the chill factor had already lowered to the point that my face and ears had become frozen just crossing the street. It had taken twenty minutes for my nose and other appendages to thaw once I reached the restaurant, during which time my face burned as if it were being heated by a welder's torch.

So what was I going to do now that the wind was whipping snow through the air with the force of a giant blender? There was only one solution, I decided: run for it. I yanked the glass door open and flung myself into the abyss. The impact of the wind was instantaneous. My entire body lifted until my toes barely touched the ground, and for a moment I feared I would be blown into the air like the proverbial leaf caught in a storm. Instincts took over. I slanted my body at a forty-five degree angle to the wind and began churning my legs in a bicycle motion. To my surprise, this worked well enough for me to make some progress across the street.

There was only one problem. My original objective, the hotel's rotating front door, was quickly sliding out of reach as I skidded sideways down the street. This would have been a good time to apply some of the geometry I should have learned in high school. All I knew was that I was traveling at an acute angle down the street faster than I was crossing it. At that rate, I figured there was about a fifty-fifty chance of reaching a telephone pole or some other anchor point before I was blown into the bay.

As it turned out, I needn't have worried so. The geometric angle proved just wide enough to not only let me reach the other side, but to sling me into the hotel's back entrance. As I staggered into the lounge-turned-refugee-camp, I couldn't help thinking about the chicken crossing the road analogy, but I was too tired and cold from my ordeal to pursue the thought. Years later I still cringe when someone asks about the motivations of that stupid chicken.

Weather. You can't live without it, and it can be hard to live with it when you are traveling. I have a few rules of thumb about the weather. One is to never take it for granted.

Not like I did in Finland when I was invited there to teach a class at a local university in Seinajoki. You can't imagine how delighted I was to be there. Finland had not been on my radar screen as a place I expected to visit, and I was thrilled at the prospect. I even arrived a few days early in mid-April so that I would have a chance to see Helsinki before my class started.

The temperature was quite brisk that first morning, but the sun was shining and I left my hotel with a map in hand and a sense of adventure. Within the hour, however, the sun made an unannounced detour behind some very dark clouds, and it started to rain. To make matters worse, I had been suckered by all the sunshine into believing the day would remain sunny, and I had left my umbrella back at the hotel. Dumb? Probably. A little too optimistic? Definitely. But what the heck, I told myself, it was only water. So what if I got a little wet? I needn't have worried. In no time, the rain turned white and fluffy, and I found myself in the middle of a snow storm. I no longer needed my umbrella, but I sure could have used that extra sweater I left neatly folded in my suitcase. I decided to beat a hasty retreat back to my hotel. That was when the snow morphed into hail, and not just any hail. These icy chunks were large enough to cause brain damage.

Some of you are probably thinking that I was already brain damaged to venture outside in one of the northernmost capitals in the world so ill prepared, and you might be right. But all of this -- sunshine, rain, snow, hail -- took place in less than two hours! How do you prepare for that? April may have been springtime in many parts of the world, but in Finland it felt an awful lot like winter.

But I digress. Back to the weather which can cause some rather strange hazards. One of my photographic assignments took me to Argentina, where Fe and I were invited to visit an estancia. Estancias are South American ranches where gauchos herd cattle and emulate the Marlboro Man. Our chosen ranch, the San Jose, had converted its main building into a colonial style guest house, complete with beautifully appointed bedrooms and antiques. It reminded me of one of those southern plantations from Gone With The Wind with a touch of the wild west tossed into the mix. Our driver picked us up in Buenos Aires and delivered us to the estancia by mid-morning with the promise that he would return later that afternoon. The timing was important, because we were scheduled to fly back to the States early the next day.

We were greeted by our hostess, Anna, who charmed us with her warm smile and offer to give us a buggy ride around the ranch. Sunshine was sprinkled liberally over the landscape, and wildflowers were in full bloom. We anticipated a memorable day. Memorable it would be, just not in the way we expected. I should have paid closer attention to Anna's casual remark about hoping it wouldn't rain, since her husband, Gunter, was gone for the day with the four-wheel drive truck. I noted some clouds rolling along the horizon, but they looked far away and harmless. Besides, a little rain wasn't going to spoil our good mood. I thought no more about it.

We enjoyed our buggy ride and a late morning walk down by a river, followed by a delicious lunch, followed by a downpour! Those harmless clouds had moved in with a vengeance. Should we return to Buenos Aires early, we wondered? No, Anna replied, that wouldn't be possible. It was then we learned that the seemingly harmless dirt road we had taken from the nearest town to reach the estancia became slicker than a sheet of ice when wet, making it impassable for normal vehicles. We were stuck there until Gunter returned with his four-wheel-drive truck.

Early afternoon slipped into early evening, and the rains continued unabated. There had been no word from Gunter, and Fe and I began to consider the idea that we might have to spend the night there. How, we wondered, could we possibly make our flight the next morning?

Just when we thought all was lost, Gunter arrived with all the drama of a white knight sent to rescue us from our comfortable dungeon. He even had our driver in tow, and he promised to deliver us safely to the nearby town where our car waited for us. To say we were relieved would have been an understatement, but our relief was short-lived. We soon learned that our real adventure was about to begin. First, Gunter informed us that he had been having a dispute with a neighboring estancia, and that someone had shot up the tires on his truck. That was why he'd been gone for

41

so long. He had hitched a ride with a friend to Buenos Aires to get new ones. Did I mention something about the Wild West? I suddenly had visions of cowboys on horseback with guns drawn chasing us all the way back to the city. Next, we discovered that the four-wheel-drive truck only had a front seat. That meant the four of us had to squeeze into a space built for two, or three at the most. The truck also didn't have an automatic transmission, and I ended up seated next to Gunter with my left leg straddling the gear shift on the floor. Every time Gunter shifted gears, his hand and gear shift came dangerously close to my . . . well you get the picture. It wasn't something on which I wanted to dwell.

However, those inconveniences were a mere preamble to the main event. The innocent dirt road we had to traverse was not only slick as ice, it was rounded on top and sloped away into a ditch on either side. Gunter had to inch along while he tried to keep his new tires on the crest of the road. It didn't take long, however, for the law of gravity to take over, and the truck began to slide towards one of the ditches. When that happened, Gunter violently spun the wheel in the opposite direction and quickly shifted gears. Spinning the wheel sent his elbow flying on a collision course with my jaw. I ducked in time, only to feel his large hand and gear shift slamming into those private parts I didn't want to think about. Slowly, Gunter coaxed the truck back onto the crest of the road, and we crawled forward once more. Before I could fully recover from my ordeal, however, the wheels slid sideways, and we started our pantomime all over again. This time, I was able to anticipate the flying elbow and sharp gear shift in time to avoid further injury.

A trip that lasted no more than twenty minutes when we arrived earlier that day now took over an hour, during which time I had to constantly duck the heavy blows of Gunter's elbow and contort myself into amazing positions to avoid the gear shift. In this manner, we eventually arrived in the town. I nearly wept with relief when our tires finally rolled onto hard pavement.

Some of the most dreaded words in travel go something like this. "You should have been here yesterday; the weather was gorgeous." Or, "For the past week there hasn't been a cloud in the sky." Such comments are generally offered in the midst of a steady downpour, and the weatherman is predicting several more days of the stuff. That's assuming you are someplace where an accurate weather forecast is even available. Weather plays an important role in our travel experiences. Sunny days are easy to enjoy. We look forward to them. It's those other days that can wreck havoc with our plans.

I, for one, am convinced that the sun never shines in Prague. Well, maybe a peek now and then, but that's about it. I made two trips to Prague to photograph that stunningly beautiful and historic city, and I only had four hours of sunshine to show for it. The rest of the time it was overcast skies mixed with intermittent drizzles. The first trip was in June. Summer came late. The next attempt was two years later in early October, which I'm told is the most beautiful time of the year. They call it Golden October. Winter came early.

Then there were the three days in Rio de Janeiro filled with heavy skies and rain. My only glimpse of the Christ statue on top of Corcovado Mountain was for a few brief moments one evening before the clouds closed in again. That followed four days in Brazil's Pantanal where the sun never showed its face again after the first afternoon. As a photographer on assignment, there is nothing more frustrating than flat light or rain.

Of course, there are opposite experiences, as well. I had the good fortune to arrive at the Perito Moreno glacier at the foot of the Andes in Argentina on a day when you could see forever. Just how rare was that occurrence? Here's a clue. The mountains surrounding the glacier were called the "mystery mountains," because nobody ever saw them. That day, I felt like I could reach out and brush the mountains' icy-blue peaks with my fingertips.

The Perito Moreno was quite a glacier. Hidden away among the hard scrabble and mountain peaks of Argentina's Patagonia region, it advanced in slow motion like a frozen twelve lane highway towards my lookout point. I was told it moved an inch or two per day. Huge chunks of ice calved from its face at regular intervals and thundered into the water below, where they floated away to become icebergs in Lake Argentino. The glacier's surface area was fifty miles long and two miles wide. That was greater than some of the world's most famous cities, and when I was there in the early 1990s, it was the only major glacier in the world that was still growing. Every few years its growth blocked the flow of water between two arms of Lake Argentino, causing one arm to flood the valley floor for miles. Eventually, enough water pressure would build against the ice barrier to break through, and the water would recede from the valley, leaving dead tree stumps in its wake.

There's nothing we can do about the weather, so we have to be prepared to take the bad with the good. Even in inclement weather, there are opportunities for wonderful experiences and picture-taking, if we are willing to adjust our expectations and look for compositions we might not notice on a clear day. What we see depends on how keen we are in our perceptions. Looking through a camera lens helps me immeasurably. Photography heightens my awareness of what's around me and gives me a much sharper eye for details. But powers of observation are not limited to a camera lens.

Earlier, I mentioned that I have a few rules-of-thumb about the weather. Here are two more. First, when the weather is bad, look beyond the standard tourist sites that we expect to see. Dig deeper and search for special details or unusual points of view. Explore a few side streets (after you have made sure they are safe). Look at your subject from different angles. That was what I did at the Great Wall of China in that snow storm. I embraced the solitude and shot close-ups of those guard towers that I mentioned before.

When I arrived at the Iguassu Falls in Brazil, my guide told me it was too bad I hadn't come the week before. "The weather was so beautiful," he lamented with a frown as he looked out from under his umbrella. It had been raining for the past two days. Undaunted, I grabbed my umbrella and shot some terrific close-ups of the waterfalls crashing down on the rocks just below me. The low lighting let me shoot at much slower shutter speeds than normal, and I was able to capture the motion of the tumbling water in some nice, time-lapsed photography.

My second rule-of-thumb is to never put off until tomorrow a photographic or sightseeing opportunity that you might do today. The first day of my visit to the Pantanal in Brazil taught me that. We had spent the afternoon near a small lake with an island where dozens of great white herons gathered in the trees at day's end. They flew across the lake and gracefully landed amongst their neighbors, who began to chatter with them. Soon, the air was filled with the sound of their jabbering, and the favored trees were transformed into a Christmas-white wonderland of fluttering wings. Warm, late-afternoon sunlight made the scene so radiant, I couldn't wait to begin taking pictures, but I couldn't get close enough without a boat. "Don't worry," my guide assured me, " we will take a boat out onto the lake tomorrow at this time. Today, we are going to walk around the lake." Tomorrow turned out to be overcast and gray, killing the lovely light of the previous afternoon.

No one ever accused me of being a slow learner. Remember Prague? When Fe and I arrived there for our second visit, our host took us by trolley for a day's outing in the city. It was late morning, and the sun was actually shining, causing the majestic St. Charles Bridge to bask in an unfamiliar glow. I asked if we could stop long enough for me to take some photographs of the famous landmark. Jokingly, I pointed out that it might be my only chance to photograph the bridge in sunlight. So, I took an hour's worth of glorious images, and we went on our way. Sure enough, by afternoon the clouds had rolled in like black bowling balls. The sun never appeared again.

Now it's pet peeve time. We all have a few of those when we travel. Mine involve the set routines and itineraries followed by tour guides around the world. They can be quite inflexible, just like our guide in the Pantanal who said it was the wrong day to take a boat out to the island where those herons were landing in the trees. Inflexible schedules and weather don't mix.

One of our trips took Fe and me to the Denpasar peninsula in Indonesia. Our destination was a small set of temple ruins that had stood on that plain for centuries. The driver dropped us and our guide off next to the ruins, then drove about a quarter mile down the road to a stopping point where he waited for us. The game plan was to visit the ruins, then take a leisurely stroll along a dirt road through the open fields until we reached our car. It was a lovely idea until the sky turned dark with leaden clouds that started spitting on us while we viewed the ruins. It didn't seem too bad at first, but by the time we were ready to walk down the road to our driver, it was raining harder. It would have been simple enough for our guide to signal the driver to come pick us up, but our itinerary called for us to walk down that road, so off we went.

Before long, the dirt road had been transformed into a quagmire of shoe-sucking mud. Rather than lose our shoes and socks to the goo, we decided to leave the road and walk in the field. That was definitely a bad idea. The field quickly turned into a swamp, making the road much more appealing. By now, we were getting drenched and had made only marginal progress towards the waiting car. I decided to take my chances with the goo and stepped back towards the road while carefully juggling a Nikon camera in either hand under a protective, plastic cover. Then, disaster struck. My last step before reaching the road found no bottom, and I thought I had been sucked into a black hole in space. Unbeknownst to me, there was a five foot ditch paralleling the road that was completely hidden by the rainwater. As I instantly sank up to my chest in standing water and mud, instincts took over and I shot both of my hands straight up in the air. I must have looked pretty silly in my "hands up" pose, but the quick reaction saved my cameras, if not my psyche. The guide hurried through the slosh to pull me out, and I introduced him to some colorful new words that I'm certain were not part of his English vocabulary. Wet, miserable, and smelling of mud, I stomped through the muck to the infamous car, where I sulked in the rear seat all the way back to Jojakarta. Where was it written, I fumed silently to myself, that the car couldn't return to the parking lot and retrieve its passengers during a rain storm? Was I in Alice's Wonderland after all?

My second example is nearly as bizarre. Fe and I had decided to try a river cruise in Europe. No photo assignment. Just a great time eating too much and visiting all the "ias" in Eastern Europe . . . Romania, Bulgaria, Slovakia, Serbia, Austria. You get the idea. The only exception was Hungary. I'm not sure how that one got in there.

There had been some devastating storms that had flooded many parts of Europe before we arrived for our trip, but we were fortunate. We began our trip in Romania under pleasant skies, and we quickly grew accustomed to one of the ship's little touches of hospitality. Each time we returned to the ship, crew members were waiting for us in the lobby with refreshing fruit drinks. Everyone agreed it was a nice gesture, and we all lined up as we came aboard to enjoy the refreshments.

There were still a few remnants of the recent storm systems lingering about, and one of them caught up with us in Bulgaria. It came in the form of a deluge that was so intense it reminded me of Iguassu Falls. The storm battered the roof of our bus until I thought it would cave in, and the roads quickly became flooded. Thunder boomed over our heads and lightning lit the dark skies with brilliant bolts of angry energy. My first thought was . . . could we make it safely back to our ship? Water was quickly gathering in the saturated fields where peasants could be seen frantically herding their few precious cows and donkeys into shelters. The livestock was saved, but there was little they could do about their crops of sunflowers, which were flattened by the intense wind and heavy rain.

Fortunately, our driver knew the roads and demonstrated great dexterity in navigating the flooded terrain. He brought us back to the ship without incident. Those of us in the front of the bus got off first and made a mad dash for the boat. The wind nearly blew us sideways, and the rain pummeled us until we felt like those sunflower stalks in the peasants' fields. We burst onboard with wet faces and heaving chests, thankful that we had reached our shelter without getting completely drenched. And there were our fruit drinks waiting for us on trays held by our smiling cabin crew. We all stopped inside the doorway and accepted the offered refreshments, not realizing the chaos that was about to unfold behind us. By now, everybody had exited the bus and was making a frantic dash for the boat, but the line for the fruit drinks blocked the doorway.

Imagine sixty people arriving late for church and everybody trying to forge a path inside, only to discover that the doors were locked and someone was standing on a ladder pouring water on their heads. That's pretty much what it was like. Bodies slammed into one another as they came to an abrupt halt in the rain. Voices cried out in consternation. People pressed forward in a desperate attempt to push their way onboard the ship. By the time the crew realized what had happened, several dozen angry vacationers were ready to mutiny. Space was quickly cleared, and the bedraggled troops stumbled onboard where they stood shaking themselves like over-watered terriers. Those of us who had caused the melee slunk away to our rooms in hopes that no one had recognized us.

The heavy rains made for some interesting drama on the river, as well. The flooding had raised the Danube by several feet, bringing many of the low-lying bridges nearly to eye level. Each time we approached a bridge, the captain ordered everything on the top deck stowed away and the radar equipment lowered. Then we crept forward, often clearing the underside of the bridge by such a narrow margin that we could almost reach up and touch it with our hands. We were told the cruise boats heading north from Vienna weren't so lucky. The Danube was too high for safe clearance there, and the cruises had to be delayed for several days.

Sometimes our travel guides misjudged the weather. That's what happened to Fe and me when we went bowling in the Chitwan Jungle in Nepal. Since I doubt there are any bowling alleys in Nepal, an explanation is in order. I should begin by mentioning that Chitwan is more of a forest than a jungle. You'll see why that's important in a moment. We were staying at a lodge and having a great time. One of the highlights was riding elephants through the savannahs and forests looking for rhinos and Bengal tigers. Saw lots of rhinos, but no tigers. The relationship between the elephants and rhinos was interesting. They tolerated each other as equals, and more or less ignored one other. That allowed us to approach to within a few feet of these fierce, horned animals and observe them up close from the backs of our pachyderms.

On the last afternoon, our guide suggested a ride in an open jeep into the forest for one last attempt to spot the elusive Bengal tiger. I should point out that these beasts are nocturnal, so the odds were slim. Still, we approached the ride with a sense of adventure. Perhaps, we would see another rhino or a bear. We were joined by the guide's sister and an Indian couple. As we were about to depart, I heard the sound of rolling thunder in the distance. It sounded like somebody was bowling strikes up there, and I asked our guide about it. No problem, he assured us. The storm was a long way off. Being the gullible traveler that I am, I took him at his word and left the protective rain gear for Fe, me, and my cameras back in our room.

As our jeep probed deeper and deeper into the forest, clouds formed overhead. They grew steadily darker until a light rain began to fall. The driver shifted from a leisurely pace to a faster gear. I placed my cameras under my shirt and tried not to look worried. Soon, thunder and lightning joined the melee, and the light rain turned into droplets the size of golf balls. We were quickly drenched, and the only thing that saved my cameras was a small hat that Fe had brought along for protection from the sun. What irony! The driver's pace increased from faster to frantic, and we weaved around trees along a road not much wider than a deer trail. Then it happened. No, we didn't see a Bengal tiger, although that would have been far less exciting. The wind suddenly whipped into a frenzy, thunder banged overhead, rain pelted us with the consistency of a waterfall, lightning snapped at our heels, and fifty foot trees began tumbling down around us like bowling pins.

We leaped from the jeep and huddled beside it while the guide's sister began screaming that we were going to die. I thought it strange that she screamed in English, but I knew she might be right. Trees continued to crash to the ground all around us; one thumped down not twenty feet away. Thankfully, the wind quickly dropped from gale force to a level one associates with hats flying through the air, and the rain settled into a steady downpour that no longer seemed intent on drowning us. Best of all, the guide's sister stopped screaming.

We found ourselves surrounded by downed trees and pools of water. Our forest had become a swamp, and our deer path was hopelessly blocked by all the fallen timber. Despite the threat of more falling trees, the guide urged us to begin walking as quickly as possible towards a ranger's station that was located about a mile away. I could tell from his furtive glances and worried frown that it wasn't falling trees that concerned him. This puzzled me until I remembered that we were in the middle of a forest filled with wild bear, rhinos, boars, and Bengal tigers. This was not the time to meet our first tiger!

We slogged through the water and mud for a good twenty minutes before we caught sight of the ranger's station. At that point I spotted several large boar staring at us from a nearby clearing. I supposed they were too surprised to attack us, but I wasn't going to stick around to find out. Miraculously, we all came through the ordeal, which I likened to survival training. This took place in the days before reality television programming, but I have a pretty good idea what it must be like to be on one of those shows. One thing I knew for certain. I would never again believe a guide who said "no problem."

But I did! Which shows I'm not only gullible but stupid. This time, our survival test took place in Tortuguero, Costa Rica, where we were scheduled to climb a large rock near our lodge. Before I describe our adventure, a little context is needed. Tortuguero really *is* a jungle, or at least a rain forest, one filled with sloths, cappuccino monkeys, and caiman. The terrain is flat, much like the Amazon. There are lots of hundred foot trees, but that's about it. So, when a rock mountain sticks its nose above the canopy, it's a big deal. This thing looked like Ayers Rock in the Australian outback, except it was surrounded by rain forest instead of desert.

Our adventure that day started innocently enough. We went on a river cruise searching for wildlife, returned for lunch, and enjoyed a relaxing nap in a swaying hammock. Then it was time to cross the river and go climb that rock. We were promised a dazzling view from the top. Once again, however, trouble loomed on the horizon. As we crossed the river, those ubiquitous black clouds began to form over our heads. I know what you're thinking. It's just me. I'm like some cartoon character who always has one of those nasty little clouds hovering above my head. You might be right.

By the time we reached the base of the rock mountain, it was starting to rain. You might think at this point that the guide would say something like "Whoops, it could get a bit slippery and muddy up there. Perhaps we should skip the climb for today." But no. Our guide wanted to keep our schedule intact and damn the torpedoes. So, he said "no problem," and we began our climb. Right off the bat I knew we were in for a memorable experience. The climb was not so much a trail as a series of boulders, vertical inclines, and tree roots to which we clung as we progressed up the mountain. And the rain quickly changed from "light showers with occasional sunshine" to the beginning of monsoon season. The hard, red clay substrate we were climbing was transformed into a slippery surface that defied our attempts to find hand holds. It was like traversing that slick road near the estancia in Argentina without the truck. We gamely continued our ascent, even as water began cascading down the trail in a series of miniature waterfalls. Somehow, we all made it to the top, but all we could see was a panorama of clouds and veils of rain. So much for the dazzling view.

It didn't take us long to decide to get out of there. When we started our descent, however, we realized that the climb down was going to go a little more "smoothly" than we had anticipated. The trail had become a combination of a water and mudslide, and the only way down was to slide on our derrières while we clung to tree trunks, fallen limbs, boulders, and anything else that presented itself. We all made it back to the bottom of the rock alive, only to discover that a new adventure awaited us. The gallons of rain water we had endured had washed off all traces of bug repellent, much to the joy of hundreds, make that thousands, of famished mosquitoes who were waiting for us. Even our rain slickers and clothing couldn't protect us. The playful little vampires punched holes right through rubber and cloth alike to get at our juicy, warm blood. By the time we returned to camp, we were soaked, skinned, and devoured, all in the quest for a view that must have been quite lovely "if you had only been here yesterday."

My last weather story is really more about Fe than myself. We had decided to take one of those cruises that begins in the Caribbean, traverses the Panama Canal, then heads north along the Mexican Riviera. It was a holiday cruise that included Christmas and New Year at sea. That pleased me because Fe's birthday was the day after Christmas, and I anticipated a nice little celebration on board ship with the crew singing happy birthday and Fe blowing out candles on a cake.

It was a small cruise ship by today's standards, and the entertainment was rather intimate. It often featured indigenous people from the countries where we docked, and on nights when that didn't happen, there were two opera singers on board who sang for us. They were both Chinese, but thankfully they didn't sing Chinese Opera, which I'd had the displeasure of hearing twice: once in Taipei and once in Beijing. Both performances consisted of high-pitched, screeching voices accompanied by a sound I could only describe as pots and pans being banged together offstage. *Our* singers had traditional opera voices. One sang for the San Francisco Opera and the other for the New York Opera. Fe and I loved their performances and always arrived early enough to sit down front.

The cruise proceeded without incident through the Panama Canal, which I have to admit was much more interesting than I thought it would be. It really was an engineering marvel, and a tragic story for the French, many of whom died of malaria while trying to build it. However, once we started up the Pacific coast, we ran into a pretty good sized storm. Our poor Chinese opera singers had never experienced such a thing. They both turned several shades of green and made it clear they were quite willing to die rather than be subjected to any further torment.

Fe rode to their rescue with dry biscuits and tea the same color as their faces. Before long, the storm subsided and our singers found their sea legs once more. Fe had become their savior.

When Christmas day arrived, I checked with our waiter about Fe's birthday surprise the next evening. He was the one surprised. He hadn't been told about it and informed me there was nothing he could do at that late date. Needless to say, I was quite disappointed. Before dinner the following evening, I happened to run into the two opera singers on deck and shared my disappointment with them. They looked at each other and told me not to worry. Something would be done.

My spirits rose, and I ate dinner with high hopes. I assumed the opera singers would arrange something with the kitchen, and while Fe and I chatted with the other couples at our table, I kept a keen eye on the waiter for some sign that everything had been arranged. But no signal was forthcoming, and by the time the desserts arrived without any cake or candles, I figured all was lost. It was then I heard voices singing off stage, and turned in time to see the two opera singers sweep into the dining room with all the drama of an opening aria. Only they weren't singing La Boheme. They were singing happy birthday to Fe with voices so brilliantly pitched, they nearly shattered all the wine and water glasses! Fe's eyes widened in disbelief, and the entire room watched with envy while Fe's new friends serenaded our table. I believe it was the best birthday present I ever gave her, and it was all made possible by some very inclement weather.

# CHAPTER FIVE
## *The Lady of the Opera*

She emerged from the crowd that flowed around the columns of Prague's National Theater following a performance of Dvorak's opera, The Devil and Kate. She was an angelic apparition dressed in a white sequined sweater, cream-colored, tailored slacks, and beige high heels with pointed toes, and she rushed across the rain-swept boulevard without an umbrella to protect her carefully coifed hair from the steady mist that saturated the night. The wet, cobblestone pavement glistened in the reflections of street lights as silver trolley car tracks snaked across the busy intersection.

A trolley was assigned to wait for those of us who did not come to the opera by car, and it sat patiently while people clambered on board to escape the poor weather. Overcoats were shaken, cold feet were stamped, and umbrellas were quickly folded. When the last customer had boarded, the doors closed with a hiss. It was then that I noticed the lady of the opera as she hurried towards the doors. They had shut before she could reach them, but a quick glance at the conductor was all she needed for them to open again. She burst into the car, breathless, with a light smile that lifted her face out of the ordinary and into a beguiling realm of elegance and charm. She was a slim woman, thirty perhaps, who effortlessly shifted her balance when the trolley stirred to life with a jarring motion. I couldn't help wondering why the lady lacked for companionship on such a moody night.

She leaned against the wall that enclosed the conductor's compartment and faced the people scattered among the car's hard, plastic seats. Her eyes flicked from one passenger to another with the whimsical movement of a butterfly flitting from flower to flower. They landed briefly on me, then moved on. At last, her eyes settled on an elderly gentlemen seated in front of her, a grandfatherly figure whose precise age was hidden behind broad shoulders cloaked in a great overcoat, the color of which matched the lady's sweater and blended with his thick mane of wavy white hair.

Soon they were engaged in familiar chatter, but the woman did not attempt to sit down. She continued to lean against the conductor's compartment and sway with the trolley's motion as if it was the most natural place to be. I didn't understand their Czech language, but I was certain they had never met before. And I didn't need a translation to know that she was slowly transforming herself from an innocent tram rider to a seductive woman. The transition was seamless. One minute she appeared to be making small talk on a lonely, wintry night; the next, her provocative body language spoke of promises as ancient as the stars. My lady of the opera had become a lady of the night.

Misty rain flowed around the tram with the mystery of a hungry fog, but she and her new companion seemed oblivious to it. She smiled as she slipped effortlessly across the social abyss that separated them. She was a siren who sang a melody of sweet words, words that brought a hearty laugh from the aging lion. He straightened his back and unconsciously brushed a wayward strand of hair from his wet face. His gaze became lost in hers. The call of the siren mesmerized him and pulled him ever closer to her rocky shore.

When she finally glided across the space dividing them and stroked the crevasses in his cheeks, it seemed only natural. She took his hand in hers and pressed it beneath her left breast, all the while continuing her silky dialog in tones of endearment and promised pleasures. At first, I thought the man might resist this unexpected onslaught of supple charms and innuendoes. He was, after all, a man of the world with decades of life's experiences to draw upon. But the lady of the opera had sparked too many youthful memories and passions. She sensed his desire and moved closer. Her cheek rested on his brow; her hands held his face; her smile glowed sweetly.

When the trolley stopped at his street, the aging lion stood up so boldly, I expected him to shake his mane and roar. But his body betrayed him. As he started towards the door, a noticeable limp slowed his progress. The lion was too old to roar, and when his new companion offered her hand to help him down the steps, he accepted it gratefully. The doors quickly closed behind them, and the trolley moved on.

If you wander through Prague's Wenceslas Square late in the evening, you will see brash prostitutes beckoning to men who wander past their webs. They are hard women without charm, wit, or style who rely on the blunt instrument of sex to attract their customers. They are strident figures, like those who surround the devil in Dvorak's opera. They lack the sensual artistry of the Lady of the Opera, who skillfully marked her prey and swept down upon him with shameless guile. I couldn't help but admire her performance, if not her profession.

Almost anywhere you travel in the world, you will find the world's oldest profession still at work in all its forms and guises. Usually, the spectacle is gritty and uninviting. Hard painted women without conscience or soul offer used beds and bodies to lonely men. Yet on a rare night, such as that one in Prague, the moment can become memorable.

As it did one night in Paris, although I almost didn't get there.

It was my first trip to Europe, my first overseas adventure. I was traveling through Europe by train, and Paris was high on my list of places to see. But to my dismay, France had gone on strike. The whole country was shut down: trains, busses, everything. It was impossible to get into the country. In fact, tour busses were transporting tourists out. Disappointed, I rearranged my itinerary but left a few days open at the end of the trip in hopes that the country would open up again before I had to return home.

Which is precisely what happened. I was in Sweden when I heard the good news, and I immediately hopped on the first train to Paris. Thirty hours later, I arrived in the city of my dreams. There I was, a tourist in Paris, but it seemed I was the only one. The city had a deserted feeling about it. I only met two other tourists during my three days there. One was from Canada and the other from Japan. Not only had the tourists fled the country, the French had as well. They had all gone on holiday until things sorted themselves out.

Remnants of the strike were still evident. Sirens blared through the city day and night as the police hurried to the next trouble spot, and university students were still protesting in the east bank. There just weren't many people. The restaurants were less than half full. The only public transportation operating was the subway system, and it stopped running at midnight. Hotels were empty.

There were benefits to being nearly the only tourist in Paris. The maitre d' and waiters at the restaurants were delighted to see me. Service was great. And when I attended an evening's performance of the famous Moulin Rouge, there were less than a dozen people in the audience. I had no problem getting a good seat. I also had my pick of hotel rooms at bargain rates. When I asked for a room at a hotel near the train station, the manager nearly wept with joy. I was his only customer. It was the only time during my trip when I didn't have to go down the hall to use the bathroom. But I must confess that I was a bit confused when I found a second porcelain fixture adjacent to my toilet. Unlike the toilet bowl, this one had no lid on it, and when I turned the knob, water shot up in the air! I had never encountered a bidet before, and I stayed as far away from that one as I could.

So, what has all this got to do with memorable moments involving women of the night? Following the Moulin Rouge performance, I decided to wander down the garish and brightly-lit boulevard of Rue Pigale, better known as Pig Alley. The tourists might have vanished, but there were still plenty of brash, young sailors on the prowl. They wandered up and down the boulevard with drinks in their hands and raucous women seated on their shoulders. The sailors bellowed with laughter and the women shouted with delight as they were carried from one bar to the next.

When I stepped into the side streets, however, an amazing transformation took place. Bright lights quickly yielded to dark alleys cloaked in dim street lamps. At first, the streets appeared empty, but as my eyesight adjusted to the faint light, I saw shadowy figures in nearly every doorway. The air seemed heavier there, the mood less buoyant. A damp odor that spoke of foggy nights permeated the air. These were truly women of the night, and they were all business. They stepped forward one-by-one and beckoned to me with soft voices as I passed. The faint light revealed empty smiles and slightly clad bodies. The scene reminded me of the movie Irma la Douce starring Shirley McClain.

The garish lights and the rough and tumble scenes along the Rue Pigale were memorable enough, but it was those mystery laden back streets that I found especially intriguing. I carried vivid memories of them for years.

Fe and I returned to Paris years later, and I couldn't wait to show her the wonderfully outlandish world of Rue Pigale. But two decades had passed, and my bright memories had faded. The sailors and their playmates were gone, replaced by lines of tour busses, choking traffic, and honking horns. The side streets were empty and well-lit. Their former occupants had retreated into crowded bars, and the sailors' uniforms had been replaced by business suits. Irma la Douce had vanished along with the pithy world I had discovered there years before. The world had moved on.

I think it's safe to say that some of our most poignant travel memories include people. In Chapter Three I talked about learning to breathe in another language. That really plays an important role with people: observing them, meeting them, and interacting with them. I call these "close encounters of the human kind." The Lady of the Opera is a great example. Here are some more.

While on photo assignment in Bhutan, I came across peasants plowing a field, and I began taking pictures of them. Bhutan is located across the Himalayas from Tibet, and the two countries have much in common. Both are Buddhist, and both believe in Bon spirits, which include spirits found in inanimate objects. Both turn prayer wheels and hang prayer flags designed to release peace and goodwill into the world, and both pray endlessly at their monasteries in preparation for their next life. Yaks are the primary beast of burden in these two countries, and both burn butter lamps at their shrines.

One major difference is altitude, which I briefly discussed in chapter three. Tibet is tucked up against the Himalayas and a few other stratospheric mountain ranges. The result is a country that starts at twelve thousand feet and rises from there. I have already mentioned the mountain passes that frequently rise above 16,000 and 17,000 feet and the lack of rainfall. The Tibetan plateau looks like a desert that got thrown like a tossed salad up among the world's highest mountain ranges. By contrast, Bhutan sits at approximately seven thousand feet and has a relatively lush landscape. Creeks and streams are abundant, and the Bhutanese have shown their ingenuity by placing prayer wheels in many of these streams where the running water turns them 24/7.

Okay, back to the peasants plowing their field. The men were guiding wooden plows pulled by great, wooly yaks, just like the Tibetans, and even at seven thousand feet, it was hard work. I noticed one woman dressed in a traditional wraparound garment called a *kira* carrying a large vessel of water for the men. Bhutan's king required both men and women to wear their national costumes at that time, the wraparound *kira* for women and a robe, called a *go,* for men. The king worried that tourism and other outside influences would dilute Bhutan's culture; he believed wearing the traditional forms of dress helped his country maintain its national pride and traditions.

The woman delivering water to the men in that field was very colorful, and I began to photograph her from a distance. As soon as she saw my camera, she stopped and began to pose for me. In fact, she became a one-act show. She placed the water vase on her head, held it at her side with a silly grin, and even performed a little dance with it. I couldn't imagine why she was so enthused, but I fired away and captured several wonderful shots. When I had finished, she hurried up to me and began looking for the pictures. It was then that I realized somebody before me had taken photos with a Polaroid camera, and she expected to see copies of her antics. This was before digital cameras became popular, and I was shooting slides. I had nothing to show her. When I pointed to the camera and shook my head no, her face fell in disappointment. I scrunched up my own face to show how sorry I was, at which point she gave me a sad little smile and headed back to the men.

In Tuscany, Italy, there's a small, walled town called Buonconvento. The town is pretty typical of that region. It seems every historic city and village is surrounded by high walls that protected its occupants during medieval times. It's easy to digress about Tuscany, where carefully trimmed cypress trees surround every farmhouse, and the earth is the color of iron. Rolling hillsides, dazzling displays of sunflowers, vineyards lined up with military precision, and rolled up wheat stalks that remind me of giant snails complete the landscape. Then there are the cities. Florence and Siena leap to mind. The Been There Done Thats will have visited them, but how about San Gimignano, whose outcrop of ancient, stone towers bristles above the town's tiled roofs? The town is famous for its towers, but my favorite memory of the place is an old man with flowing white hair and wire-rimmed glasses sitting in his musky bookshop and pouring over an old manuscript with the keen interest of a bibliophile.

It was a very "human" moment, and that brings me back to Buonconvento, a five block village with one narrow main street that curved past a small clock tower and rows of tired, brick buildings. There was little to attract tourists to the town. Most people rushed past Buonconvento without a second glance as they searched for Tuscany's more famous landmarks, but I was captivated by the stone archway that framed the town's main entrance and the massive wooden door that had once guarded it. Fe and I decided to stop and have a look around. It took less than thirty minutes to explore the main street and its offshoots. Potted plants and a few freshly-painted window frames brought some life to the aging buildings. Three bottles of red wine sat on a windowsill in the thin sunlight. The streets and sidewalks were swept clean. You could see that the residents took pride in their village, but other than an interesting shop or two, there wasn't much to hold us there.

Outside the arched entrance a small garden filled with struggling plants and sparse rose bushes surrounded a simple, stone fountain. A circular walkway and several benches completed the scene. Behind the garden the mottled wall that guarded the town showed the corrosive markings that come from centuries of storms and wear. The place seemed weighed down by its own history.

We were about to leave when a gardener with clippers in one hand and a trowel in the other walked into the colorless setting. He began to meticulously prune a rose bush near the front gate by grasping each thorny stem with a bare hand and clipping old stock away just above a new green nub of growth. A few bees buzzed around him with interest, but he ignored them just as he ignored the thorns pricking his fingers.

Fe is the gardener in our family, and she stepped closer to watch him work. His meticulous efforts showed his concern for those struggling plants. Each one was carefully inspected, then snipped and trimmed of dying blossoms and unsightly stems. When he saw Fe, he smiled, said something in Italian, pointed at some rust colored leaves, and shook his head. We didn't need Italian to understand that the plants had been invaded by aphids and were not doing well. Time seemed of little importance to the gardener. He moved slowly and made each cut with the precision of a surgeon. It was inspiring to watch his singular effort to gain a foothold of color and beauty in that drab landscape. We assumed he was employed by the town, but it was apparent that there was more to his reward than a salary. The rose garden was his canvass, and while its bloom may have faded, it didn't stop the artist from continuing to work in his chosen medium.

We discovered other human touches during our drive through Italy, including a nun at Assisi who sat on the chilly ground at the base of the old castle wall overlooking the famed basilica and city. She had wrapped herself in her thin habit while she meditated, but the habit afforded poor protection against the bracing wind that scoured her exposed position. Even inside my warm jacket I could feel the bite of that sunless wind, but when I approached the nun and indicated she could borrow it for awhile, she shook her head emphatically and returned to her prayers. It seemed that suffering in the cold was part of her penance, and I could not help but admire her dedication. Fe and I explored the area for over an hour, during which time she never moved.

Such brief encounters and visual vignettes provide memories and images beyond the usual travel fare of monuments, religious shrines, and city streets. It's the people who make up the heart and soul of the travel experience. It's the people who help us learn to breathe in another language.

I have already mentioned my first trip to China, which took place in the wintertime. It was the mid 1980s, and many of the older people still wore their Mao jackets and trousers, which quite frankly reminded me of prison garb. The clothes were a dull, blue-grey color and shapeless in design. I guessed that some wore them to keep warm, but I also suspected that many wore them because they wanted to save money. The economic boom enjoyed by China today had not yet begun, and many older folks had little money, a situation that was confirmed when an elderly gentleman began to walk and talk with me while I wandered the streets of Guilin. Picking up a walking companion was common in those days. The locals were delighted to meet foreigners, and it gave them an opportunity to practice their English. I learned that my new friend was a retired architect who had lived a relatively comfortable life by Chinese standards at that time, but now he had to get by on a small, government stipend. He spent his days seated on a stool in front of his tiny house where he watched a newer China passing by him. After we had walked awhile, we entered a quiet street and were momentarily alone. My companion glanced nervously about, then stepped closer and asked in a low voice if I could spare a few yuan so that he might cover the difference between his meager pension and his rising expenses. His eyes continued to dart furtively up and down the empty street. It was obvious he didn't want his neighbors to see him begging. He was torn between his need for money and his fear of losing face. In the end, his need for money won out, and when I discreetly slipped him a few yuan, his face reddened with gratitude. I watched him sadly as he bowed and hurried away. He was a proud, educated man, now reduced to the painful practice of looking for handouts in a world that was changing beyond his understanding or control. I had no idea how long he'd resorted to this embarrassing behavior, but I was pretty sure his neighbors knew about it. Something like that would be hard to hide in such a close-knit community. They said nothing, of course, because they didn't want him to lose face, either.

It's amazing to realize how far China has come since my walk with that retired architect. Twenty-five years ago, hints of the future were already evident in Shanghai's skyline. Gleaming, new high rise office buildings and hotels were soaring into the air; construction boomed day and night. It never stopped. Still, change would take some time. Nearly everyone rode bicycles in those days. They poured out of side streets and filled every intersection. Everywhere I went, the streets were clogged with a steady stream of two-wheeled commuters. And the Mao jackets could still be found.

One of the most telling episodes of just how far the Chinese have come occurred near the famous Wuxing Ting Tea House, an elegant, old wooden building of polished teakwood that was surrounded by a pond filled with plump, gaily-colored goby fish. Pedestrian bridges were used to reach the place, but the bridges were built in a zigzag fashion that made it impossible to walk directly to the tea house. Why were the bridges built that way? To prevent evil spirits from reaching the sanctuary. The Chinese believed spirits moved in straight lines and couldn't negotiate the bridge's sharp, left-right turns. Culture moved at a glacial pace compared to the building of those skyscrapers.

My desire to breathe in another language led me down some of the surrounding streets. As I walked, I came upon a little boy playing with a ball on the sidewalk next to a fire hydrant. His father stood nearby watching him. I gestured to the father with my camera and knelt down to take the boy's picture. What a little ham he turned out to be! He immediately dropped the ball, squatted on his haunches, and began playing with a chain attached to the fire hydrant. The father and I both laughed as I took his picture, and the boy grinned with pleasure.

The boy's impromptu pose took me by surprise, but a greater surprise awaited me when I ran out of film. A few dozen residents had observed me photographing the boy while they went about their chores. One woman was raising wet laundry with a stick to a wire overhead where it could hang and dry. A man whittled a thin piece of wood to slide into a gap in his windowsill so the cold wind couldn't invade his house. Everybody was busy, but the moment I opened my camera to change the roll of film, they stopped what they were doing and headed towards me with curious smiles. Others further down the street saw the commotion and hurried to join them. In less time than it took to say Kodak film, a crowd of forty people had gathered around me, all murmuring and pointing at my camera. There I was, five blocks from one of the most famous landmarks in one of the biggest cities in China, yet those folks acted like they had never seen anyone changing film before! They reminded me of that woman in Bhutan who expected pictures to magically appear from my camera. The Chinese were very polite, I never felt threatened, and when I had finished changing the film, they quickly dispersed.

What would happen if I returned to that street today, I wonder? I imagine many of those folks would take pictures of me with their digital cameras and download them on their computers!

Children are always a delight to photograph. One in Sulawesi, Indonesia, caught me just as off guard as those people in Shanghai. Fe and I were walking down a country road that cut across a lush field when I noticed an old, wooden outhouse straddling a small stream. Curious, I approached the unpainted structure just as the door popped open and a little girl of five or six emerged from the outhouse without a stitch of clothing. I don't know who got the bigger shock, her or me. She froze in the doorway just long enough for me to raise my camera and capture her in her moment of confusion. She looked like a blossoming flower in morning sunlight, and her pose standing in that doorway was priceless. After she was gone, I took a peak inside and found what I feared. There was no receptacle of any kind. Only a round hole cut in the floor boards above the little river, which acted as a naturally flushing toilet. I didn't want to think about what the water was used for downstream.

While we're on the subject of children, Fe and I happened to be in Mexico City while a band of Ciapas Indians was protesting the government's treatment of its poor, indigenous citizens. They had set up a tent city right in the middle of the Zocalo, which was the main square in front of the government building that housed President Salinas' offices. The Zocalo was filled with yellow, green, and orange plastic shelters and canvass tents, all set against a backdrop of government buildings and the city's famed Cathedral. It was a colorful sight. At dusk, thousands of demonstrators from all over Mexico marched into the square carrying brightly painted protest banners in defiance of the government's order for the Indians to disband and return to their province. The marchers gathered in the square while the Ciapas Indians danced in their native costumes. The natives formed a circle that widened as several tourists joined them. Together, they swayed to the constant beat of drums well into the night.

Naturally, I photographed like crazy, but of all my shots, one stood out with a clarity of message that none of the others could muster. It was the image of a little girl poking her head through a wall of protest banners in the middle of the square and beaming a broad, innocent smile at the world. I couldn't help thinking of the biblical reference about a child leading them. Her smile, framed by those banners, held out more hope than all the marchers and protest banners combined.

You can see how such encounters can enrich our travel experiences. There was one occasion, however, when Fe and I thought we had slipped into a twilight zone. It all started with a boat ride on the Nile River in Egypt. What an amazing river! With its tributaries, the Nile flows through nine countries and is claimed to be the longest river in the world. Amazon enthusiasts will quarrel with that claim, but nobody can doubt that the Nile was one of the great cradles of history.

The Luxor region alone offers one of the most amazing collections of antiquities found anywhere in the world. There is Abu Simbel, a massive temple dedicated to the sun god, Ra, built by Ramses ll. The Egyptians had to dismantle it stone-by-stone and reassemble it 180 miles away to save it from flooding when the Aswan Dam was built. Then, there is the Luxor Temple and neighboring Karnak, a sprawling complex of temples less than two miles away. There used to be an avenue lined with hundreds of sphinx-shaped lions connecting the two temple sites. Over the centuries, buildings and city streets have encroached on most of the route, but some of these magnificent sculptures can still be seen at both temple sites. Archeologists have uncovered more than sixty of them to date.

Then there are two of the most famous valleys in the world: the Valley of the Queens and the Valley of the Kings. Wow. Many of Egypt's great pharaohs and queens were buried there in chambers dug deep into the hillsides. Nearly every inch of the long, narrow passageways leading down to the tombs was originally covered with brilliantly painted hieroglyphics, gods, and royal images. The artwork in some of the shafts has been so well preserved, you would think it had been painted yesterday.

So, what has all this got to do with entering the twilight zone? During our visit to the Luxor region, we traveled up and down the Nile on a small cruise ship. Everywhere we went we saw dozens of these floating hotels plying the placid waters, and every evening they jostled for space along the docks where we all stopped for the night. There were far more ships than docking spaces, so the boats tied up along side each other and passengers on the outer boats had to traipse back and forth through the lobbies of the adjoining ones which were docked closer to shore. We often saw as many as five boats tied together in this manner.

Until we stopped at Qena. Qena is a city of considerable size, yet we were the only ship docked there. After the buzz of activity that had surrounded us at the other stops, it was downright eerie to suddenly be so alone. We learned that Qena had once been the center of uprisings against Mubarak's government, and it was the city where Osama bin Laden's top advisor, al-Zawahiri, started his own revolutionary movement before joining al-Qaeda. Qena's history gave me pause.

We were assured by our tour operator that we were perfectly safe, but when we asked if we could wander into the city on our own, we were advised not to. So why the heck were we there? It turned out that our tour operator provided financial support for a girl's school in Qena, and we were going to visit it the next morning. But first, we were going to enjoy some local entertainment in the city that night. To get there, we boarded a child-sized, wooden train with no walls or roofs and rode for twenty minutes through empty streets so heavily guarded by armed police, I thought we had invaded Iraq. Traffic at every cross street was blocked, as well, so we didn't have to slow down at intersections. It was better, I supposed, to remain moving targets! The children waved as they always do, and many of the women smiled. Some men greeted us with nods of their heads. Most simply stared after us, with curiosity or caution I couldn't tell. I felt as though we were riding through a haunted forest, and I half expected the headless horseman to appear at any moment.

After enjoying what turned out to be a very good show, we hopped back into the open cars of our little, wooden choo-choo and returned to the ship. Again, we were whisked along streets with no traffic and sped past blocked intersections, all under the watchful eye of the police. The next day, we repeated the ritual all over again, only this time in a tour bus. Visiting the girl's school was a treat, but I had to admit that I wasn't disappointed when we returned to our ship, slipped the ropes from our moorings, and headed out into the Nile River. My mettle had been tested enough; I wanted to get out of there!

The first time I had my mettle tested was many years ago when I had to endure the highly ritualized customs and immigration process required to enter Burma, now called Myanmar by the military dictatorship that runs the place. I'm not sure calling it an immigration process quite captures the experience. It was more like a quest for the holy grail. There were five of us traveling in a mini-group from Thailand, and when we landed in Rangoon, we were immediately herded into a small processing room along with everyone else on our flight. The room was just big enough to accommodate us. I mention this because, while it wasn't summer, it felt like Florida on the Fourth of July, and there was no air conditioning. The heat in the room had to be pushing one hundred degrees and the humidity was so close to hundred percent, there were weather systems forming on the ceiling. To put it another way, if the humidity had been any higher, it would have been raining in there.

We all sort of milled around in this self-imposed steam bath while we smelled each other's deodorants (or lack thereof) and looked for any semblance of an organized line. We did this for the better part of an hour, during which time we made only marginal progress towards a counter where two officials were processing the visas. Sweat was no longer pouring down my brow. It was drowning me. I began to think of us less as tourists and more like cattle waiting to be branded.

The visa process was amazing to watch. An official would take someone's passport and begin turning the pages one at a time. He would stare at each page for upwards of a minute, then slowly turn to the next page. This ritual was repeated until the entire passport had been scrutinized. Once the official was through with the passport, he began to pour over the visa application. This took nearly as long as reviewing the passport. By the time he had finished with both, ten minutes had passed, and if anything on the visa application was found to be incorrect, the poor applicant had to rectify the mistake and return to the back of the group.

I figured that at our rate of progress, it would take us seven days just to get through customs. Since seven days was the length of time allowed on the visa, we might not technically ever enter the country. We would simply languish there until it was time to board our plane and return to Bangkok. That was assuming there were no errors in our visa applications. Okay, I admit I'm exaggerating a bit, but that was how I felt.

It was time to act boldly. At the airport in Bangkok, everybody had purchased two cartons of a brand of cigarettes called 555 and two bottles of Johnny Walker Red whisky. These items were considered more valuable than money in Burma and could be used to bribe officials. I turned to my travel companions and asked them to give me their passports along with two packs each of 555 cigarettes. With booty in hand, I stepped forward and placed each passport on the counter face up. Next, I boldly placed two packs of 555s on top of each passport. Then I stepped back, and waited. Nothing happened. The officials ignored me and my bribes. I had only made matters worse, my inner voice scolded me. I shouldn't have been so blatant. Now, I was certain we would never get out of that steaming building, and my clammy body sweated some more.

Then a miracle occurred. A hand suddenly shot out and swept the cigarettes into a container under the counter. The official's hand moved with the speed of a rattlesnake's tongue. One moment the cigarettes were neatly stacked on the counter, the next they were gone. My smile was a wry combination of relief and triumph. Diplomacy worked. Bribes worked. Minutes later, we were motioned to the counter and our passports and visa applications reviewed with a brisk efficiency heretofore unseen. The officer even found an error in my visa application, but to my delight he corrected it on the spot and waved us into his country. I'm willing to bet that after our little group was gone, a lot more packs of 555 cigarettes began appearing on that counter.

Not all close encounters of the human kind are that dramatic. In the city of Augsberg, Germany, there's a tiny, walled village called Fuggerei where poor people can live for a few Euros per year. There are three qualifying requirements to live there. You have to be an Augsberg citizen, Catholic, and flat broke. Fuggerei's one claim to fame is that Mozart's great grandfather lived there. The village isn't much bigger than a postage stamp, and the setting is perfectly suited for pixies and leprechauns. Narrow stone streets and vine-covered buildings fill the handful of blocks that comprise the village, and a fountain tinkles in a small square. Four archways in the exterior walls, like the four points of a compass, allow residents and visitors to come and go. Otherwise, the compact village is tucked away so quietly behind the surrounding streets, someone walking past might not even realize it was there.

Fe and I were wandering on foot through this Lilliputian realm when an old woman with a scrubbed, cherub face and winsome smile emerged from her home. I wanted to take her picture, but she demurred. Then, Fe struck up a conversation with her, even though the woman spoke no English and Fe spoke almost no German. That, by the way, has always been one of my wife's many fine qualities. She makes friends everywhere she goes, including with people who don't give me a second glance, and that often opens doors for my photography.

Sure enough, Fe's diplomacy soon had the elderly lady so enthralled, she opened *her* door and invited us into her world, a world that consisted of three miniature rooms -- sitting room, kitchen, and bedroom -- all meticulously clean and arranged like some of those cordoned-off rooms you see in museums. There was barely room for the three of us to turn around, but to her it was paradise, and her back straightened with pride as she showed it to us. She even invited me to take pictures, then posed with Fe for that elusive photograph of her. Our time spent together was less than a quarter of an hour, but we will always remember our Fuggerei friend.

Fe and I had another warm and fuzzy encounter when we drove through Yugoslavia before the country splintered so violently into its separate parts. Wherever possible, we traveled back roads so that we could enjoy the countryside and observe the local people going about their daily lives. On a small road leading from Zagreb to Banja Luka, we encountered a peasant woman walking down a path to her house. She was dressed in a colorful skirt and rugged, white shirt, and her head was covered with a knitted shawl. Naturally, I stopped the car and hopped out to take her picture. When she saw my camera, she stood proudly in the center of the path and gave me a broad smile. She was so delighted at the idea of having her picture taken, I thought for a moment I was back in Bhutan shooting that peasant woman. I was checking my f-stop and shutter speed when I heard a woman cry out, and I looked up with alarm, thinking something had happened. It turned out to be the woman's neighbor, who had been seated in front of her house. When she saw what I was doing, she jumped to her feet and shouted for me to wait while she rushed up the road. I wouldn't have described either woman as slim, and by the time the neighbor had joined her friend, her chest was heaving as she labored to catch her breath. The two women stood side-by-side holding hands and grinning like smiling fence posts. Normally, I try to avoid poses, but there was something about the two of them that made that one work. I think it was their enthusiasm and their rapport with each other. It was apparent that they rarely saw tourists, and they were delighted to share the moment together.

Of course, there is one sort of human encounter you do your best to avoid. I'm talking about pick-pockets and purse snatchers. Some cities are famous for them. In Naples, thieves ride motor scooters and slice purse straps with a sharp knife as they pass women on the street. In a heartbeat, the purse is gone, and so are they. Rome is also famous for pick-pockets.

In all our years of travel we have never lost a dime. One reason is that we try to stay aware of our surroundings and use reasonable precautions, such as keeping our valuable documents and money in pouches hidden inside our clothing. We never carry wallets or wads of money in our pockets.

We have had our share of near misses, however. Once, Fe and I were leaving the Louvre in Paris at closing time when we were accosted by a begging gypsy woman. She kept trying to intercept us and block our path, and I kept veering away from her. Finally, I yelled at her, and after a moment's hesitation she let us pass. When Fe asked why I had gotten so angry, I told her something just had not felt right. I'd never seen a gypsy begging in Paris before. When we returned to the U.S., we saw a report on 60 Minutes about gypsy women stopping tourists and children swarming them and stealing all their valuables. One of the most popular spots was outside the Louvre at closing time!

But even the most savvy traveler is bound to get waylaid sometime. That's what happened to me in Poland. We had been warned that the thieves there worked in groups at the train stations. The Warsaw and Gdansk stations were particularly bad. Their system was really quite simple. One thief created a distraction while the others nimbly picked all your pockets. That is exactly what they did to me at the train station in Krakow. We had already made it through Warsaw and Gdansk without incident, and I guess I let my guard down. I was about to lift the first of two suitcases onto the train when a nicely dressed man appeared in the doorway and lifted it inside for me. With the second suitcase in hand, I followed him onto the train and tried to retrieve the first one, but he kept lifting it up in the air as if he intended to put it in an overhead rack. Then he would put it down again. I finally grabbed it away, and he disappeared out the door. It was only then that I realized what had happened. Fe told me four men had boarded the train behind me and frisked me while I tried to reclaim the suitcase.

I never felt so much as a finger on me, but I had no doubt that they had searched my pockets thoroughly. Fe and I quickly checked our hidden pouches. The valuables and money were safe. Nor had the suitcases been opened. The pick-pockets left empty handed, and I breathed a huge sigh of relief.

After so much excitement, it seems appropriate to end this chapter on a humorous note. Many years ago, I took a scenic boat ride down the Li River in China with a client. There was a large observation deck on the second level that allowed us to admire some truly dramatic scenery. Morning mists wafted across the water, partially obscuring the dozens of mountain peaks shaped like giant stalagmites which rose into the sky around us. Peasants stood on tiny rafts fashioned from tree trunks and harvested something that looked like seaweed from the river bottom with bamboo poles. Bigger rafts ferried bicycles and their owners from one bank to the other.

The river narrowed until the prehistoric mountain peaks towered above our heads, and the mists added an air of mystery to the languid setting. Thoughts wandered. Time became lost in the river's twists and turns.

Then all Hell broke loose. We were approaching a loading dock where dozens of merchants waited for us in tiny boats. The merchants quickly surrounded our vessel and beckoned us with urgent voices to buy their postcards and souvenirs. Others waited on the shore, their strident voices drowning the blissful silence we had enjoyed for the past hour.

We asked the boat captain about the situation and received some good news and bad news. First the good news. The merchants were not allowed onboard the boat. Now the bad news. We would return to the same dock when it was time to disembark. A walkway of wooden planks lying across a muddy field defined the route we would have to take to reach a nearby village where our car waited for us. I estimated the distance to be a quarter of a mile, and I tried to imagine negotiating those slippery boards to the bus with all those merchants yelling and yapping at our heels. It would be the equivalent of running a gauntlet through a pack of hungry wolves.

Then, a Japanese tour group came to our rescue. We stopped to pick them up a little further down the river, and they swarmed up the stairs to the observation deck's railings with the same gusto as commuters boarding a Tokyo subway. In less time than it took to say *youkoso* (welcome!), every spot along the rails was taken. They were so aggressive, I almost missed the Chinese merchants awaiting our return. So, how did the Japanese rescue us? The captain told me they would leave the boat where we did, and I suspected they would do so with the same "damn-the-torpedoes" spirit they had demonstrated while boarding. When we reached the dock, I suggested to my client that we hang back and let the Japanese group leave first. With a little luck, they would blaze a trail for us through all those maniacal merchants. And that's exactly what they did. The boat docked, and the Japanese stormed off so quickly you would have thought it was sinking. They were instantly surrounded by the merchants who chased them all the way across that muddy field with the fury of bees protecting their hives. Two members of the tour group were even bumped off the wooden planks into the muddy goo. A few minutes later, my client and I enjoyed a leisurely stroll to our car. We hopped inside before the merchants even realized we were there.

# CHAPTER SIX
*Confessions of a Key Collector*

We all have an obsession or two about collecting souvenirs, don't we? Well, I know some of us do, and when we travel this can take some bizarre twists. I've heard of people collecting silverware from restaurants, hair shampoo bottles from hotels, even bathrobes from the finer establishments. However, I've never heard of anyone else with my obsession: collecting hotel keys. It's not so much the key; its the key tag. Some of the tags, particularly those from hotels in foreign countries, are works of art. They can be circular, triangular, rectangular, and every other shape imaginable. Materials include plastic, metal, leather, and wood, and some of the designs are to die for. Once you start down the path leading to the dark side, it's easy to get caught up in this pursuit. I know what you're thinking. How do you keep the hotel key tag when you check out? Most hotels have an unreasonable desire to hang onto the things, and they keep a pretty close eye on them. The answer enters the realm of pure artistry. I mean, we're talking about the imagination and boldness of a cat burglar here.

I suppose I should explain how this whole thing got started. When I was a relatively innocent teenager, I dined with my parents at a restaurant in Los Angeles called the Original Bar-B-Q. There on the table in front of me was an ash tray that stated in bold, brash lettering, "I stole this ashtray from the Original Bar-B-Q." What could I do? I was fifteen. My hormones were running riot. Of course, I took it, and thus began my slippery slide into the underworld of crime. This was back in the days when everyone still smoked in restaurants, so game was plentiful. Soon, I was collecting ashtrays from all over Los Angeles. I even had friends bringing me ones they had taken on my behalf. It wasn't long before I had three boxes filled with those glass and ceramic things. Which raised a logistical problem. What the heck was I going to do with all those ashtrays? Not only was I becoming overwhelmed by them, but I was starting to feel a bit guilty. Eventually, common sense was restored, and I ditched my budding collection in the trash. What a relief. I felt free and unencumbered.

At least I thought I was free and unencumbered. Little did I realize how foolish and naïve I was. Little did I realize that my passion for collecting travel items would soon leap to a higher level. After I graduated from college, I began traveling around the country on business, and I soon had a small box filled with key tags. The tags were mostly made of cheap, plastic material, and nobody bothered to ask for them when I checked out.

When you begin collecting on a global scale, however, the task becomes much more challenging. Foreign hotels often have far more artistic key tags, and as I mentioned before, they watch them closely. So, the need for stealth and cunning was born. Today, I have over a hundred and twenty-five dazzling key tags collected from over fifty countries around the world, many from exotic locations like Burma, Uzbekistan, Bora Bora, Borneo, Turkey, Jordan, and Tibet. They hang like hunting trophies around the borders of a world map that graces a wall in my office. It seems to be a unique collection. I have yet to meet anyone with a similar accumulation.

So, how does one go about collecting hotel keys? Many approaches can be used. I discovered, for example, that many Europeans leave their keys dangling in the outside of the door locks when they leave. Fe and I once stayed at a new hotel on a cliff overlooking the medieval walled city of Dubrovnik in what was then Yugoslavia. What a magnificent sight! We sat on the balcony at dawn and watched the sun kiss the red-tiled rooftops and stone church steeples of the ancient, walled city as it woke from its slumber. Below us, small fishing vessels chugged quietly out to sea. It was a scene of timeless splendor. Later that morning, we wandered along the top of Dubrovnik's walls and watched people at eye level as they hung laundry from third story windows or read a book in the sunlight. Then, we plunged down into the cobblestone streets below, where deep shadows accented the labyrinth created by narrow passageways and high walls. Children played with their small toys and pets along the stone alleyways, their squeals echoing off the walls, and a man stripped off his shirt to bathe in an outside fountain, unperturbed by passersby.

Okay, let's get back to the main topic before I get carried away. The hotel's key tag was round and comprised of a combination of clear plastic and brass. It had a colorful design on one side and the room number set in gold letters against a field of red on the other. Be still my heart! I wanted that tag, but I knew the hotel staff would represent formidable opposition. They would want it back when we left. Two days passed without incident, and I had more or less given up on the idea of capturing one of those gems. Then, fate intervened. On the morning we were to check out, I was walking down the hall to our room when I stopped in wonder. There was a key dangling from the door lock just three rooms from ours. I was ecstatic and quickly retrieved my prize before the hotel staff discovered it was missing. Sadly, that hotel was destroyed when the Serbs shelled Dubrovnik, which makes my key tag one of a kind.

Many times I have offered to pay for the key tag without the key, and this has generated some surprising results. One time Fe and I stayed at the Mount Kenya Safari Club in Africa. The club was originally built by William Holden and some of his fellow movie stars as a private, big game retreat in Kenya. It's now a hotel with strange looking storks lurching across the lawns and Mount Kenya preening in the distance. The key had a rather plain, metallic tag attached to it, but I wanted it nonetheless. So, I went to the front desk, explained my interest, and offered to pay for an extra tag. Imagine my surprise when the young man behind the counter waved his hand and told me to wait a moment while he rummaged through a drawer. Voila! Out popped an old, wooden, oversized tag with Mount Kenya Safari Club carved on one side and a room number on the other. The tag had slid around in that drawer for who knows how many years, and now it hangs on my wall. Was it one of the tags originally made for the hotel? I would like to think so.

Another time, I traveled to the remote region of Torajaland on the island of Sulawesi in Indonesia. The area was so difficult to reach, the natives there had remained cannibals until the early 1900s when the Dutch finally pacified them. They no longer ate visitors, but they still had some extraordinary habits. They "buried" their dead in open caves or in wooden coffins that were hung from cliffs. The coffins were poorly constructed and soon fell apart, resulting in human bones and skulls tumbling to the ground. The remains were then casually stacked on fallen logs or on the ground and forgotten. Once the spirit was gone, it seemed the skeleton no longer mattered. The wealthier families paid a local craftsman to carve life-like sentries that were posted in front of the burial caves. It was believed these sentries protected the deceased from evil spirits. Rows of those brightly painted, wooden figures could be seen standing guard in the surrounding cliffs.

I stayed at a small inn, the Misiliana, which had beautiful, wooden key tags. Mine was shaped in a rectangle with a curved dome on top and rust, mustard, and white colored patterns carved, stained, and painted into the wood. The room number stood out in brilliant white against a black background. The word Misiliana had been added in white letters across its base. I immediately asked the inn's manager if I could buy one. He told me not to worry, my guide would take care of it the next day. Sure enough, the next morning we set out bright and early across the lush fields to a small village comprised of half-a-dozen long houses. The long houses were shaped like boats and were raised about ten feet off the ground to protect them from flooding during the rainy season. There, I met the artisan who had hand-carved each key tag for the hotel. He wrote down my room number and the following day presented me with my own, personalized tag. What did it cost me? I don't even remember, but I know it was a lot less than a Starbucks latte.

Bribery is another method that works quite well in certain countries. Remember those 555 cigarettes in Burma? I paid a full pack to the hotel bellman in Rangoon for a round, yellow, plastic tag with gold lettering that said Strand Hotel on it. The Strand Hotel, by the way, was one of those old English hotels left over from the British Empire. The lobby and restaurant had very high ceilings and marble floors. Sweeping fans the size of airplane propellers stirred the heavy air. Hot and humid did not begin to describe the oppressive conditions. There were window air conditioners in the rooms, but they only raised false hopes since they didn't work. And forget about running a cool bath unless you wanted to submerge yourself in sludge. There are several newer hotels in Burma today, so I expect most of the colorful lodging experiences I've just described have disappeared.

Another tactic that I used with great success was the broken key tag method. I would simply return the key and explain that the tag had broken off. That worked best at check-out time. I would offer to pay something for the lost tag, but the desk clerk was usually so pleased to get the key back that there was no charge. I used that approach at the Hong Kong Hotel in order to snag a long, rectangular, plastic tag with an artist's sketch of the Hong Kong skyline etched into it. I also obtained a leather tag in Mexico City that way, and an orange colored tag from the Patagonia Inn near Puerto Natales, Chile.

Sometimes guilt enters the equation. Not the "I wish I hadn't taken it" kind of guilt. No, I'm referring to the "I'm about to get caught" sort of guilt. That happened to me in Tashkent, Uzbekistan. I had just discovered a key left in the door of an empty room across the hall as Fe and I were leaving to see the sights. In those days, each floor was guarded by a very stout and severe looking woman who sat at a tiny desk by the elevators where she could keep an eye on things and prevent unwanted guests from visiting the rooms. As Fe and I approached the elevators, the guard on our floor eyed me with so much suspicion I was certain she had seen my slight of hand moments ago. In reality, she eyed everyone suspiciously. I suspect that was part of her job description, but that didn't prevent my imagination from running wild. By the time we had exited the building, I was feeling a bit nervous. What if I was stopped by the KGB? I actually glanced around to see if we were being followed. Nothing happened, of course, and you can imagine how silly I felt by the time we returned to the hotel. Guilt has a funny way of working on one's psyche.

By now it should be obvious that many of the key tags in my collection have interesting or humorous stories behind them, and some are special to me because of the unusual circumstances under which I got them. There are two keys, however, that are unique because of the hotel itself. The first came from Howard's Room at the Bayshore Inn in Vancouver. I was there on a business trip and had already checked in before learning that the conference room I had reserved for meetings was unavailable. The hotel manager apologized and immediately upgraded me to a suite with a living room that I could use for my purpose. That was no problem. I had used living room suites before, and I knew I would enjoy the extra space. The manager went on to say that the suite they would normally have given me was still occupied, so they were upgrading me to a larger suite at no additional cost. The deal was getting better by the minute.

The bellman retrieved my luggage and off we went. While we waited for the elevator, the bellman commented that I would be staying in Howard's House. I had no idea what he meant, but when we exited the elevator on the top floor, I saw a sign above the door at the end of the hall that said Howard's House. It turned out that I would be staying in the corner suite where Howard Hughes had been living just six months ago. I was told that wealthy travelers had been sparring with each other ever since to reserve that suite, but on that particular night, the room was empty. The suite was lovely, but it was the view of Vancouver's skyline and surrounding mountains that caught my breath. The view from Howard's House was so dramatic, it could only have been duplicated in an airplane. When I checked out the next day, I simply kept the key tag.

The other tag is from the Hotel Sir Francis Drake in San Francisco. Wait a minute, you will say. That's not from a foreign country. True enough, but it's in my collection due to its remarkable imagery and historic value. The tag is made out of metal, and the building's exterior is raised in relief from the surface. It was most likely formed by a forge, but it looks as though somebody could have chiseled it by hand. On the back side, the hotel's name is raised in a script format, and the room number is stamped into the metal. To say that the tag is old would be an understatement. Its aged appearance makes one wonder if it was forged when the hotel was rebuilt after the 1906 earthquake and fire. I've had it for forty years, and it had to be at least that old when I got it. So, I'm estimating its age to be more than eighty years. Worth keeping, don't you think?

One more confession and we're done. I confess that I took one hotel key purely out of spite. It happened while I was attending a travel conference in Bali. I was there on behalf of a tour operator, and I had made a number of appointments with land operators and hotels to review their products, services, and pricing. My last appointment was with the sales manager for an Asian hotel. When I arrived at the allotted time, the sales manager was meeting with her staff. It was obvious that she had forgotten about our appointment. She asked me to wait in the suite next door, and I complied. Twenty minutes spun by before she rushed rather rudely into the room. Her meeting was still in progress, so we had less than five minutes together before she rushed out again. She actually left me sitting there in the room. I didn't know which irked me more, her rude behavior or her cavalier attitude towards our appointment. As I got up to leave, I noticed the suite's key sitting on the table, and I couldn't help myself. I took it. That wooden key tag with blue lettering now adorns my map along with my other trophies. So beware the wrath of a key collector scorned!

What is the moral of this chapter? Watch out for collectors who travel the world in search of new treasures. Whether ash trays, bathrobes, or key tags, nothing is sacred. I must add, however, that collecting hotel key tags is becoming a dying profession. All the new hotels and many of the older ones have converted to electronic plastic cards. Some do include the hotel's name, and you are welcome to take them, but a collection of plastic cards just doesn't have the panache of those earlier works of art. A collection like mine would be difficult to duplicate today. I wonder what it would be worth on Ebay?

# CHAPTER SEVEN
## *THE "OOPS" FACTOR*

Remember way back in Chapter Two when I told the story about the automated airplane where absolutely nothing could go wrong . . . go wrong . . . go wrong? I think we've pretty much debunked that idea. Let's face it. No matter how carefully you plan your travels, something is bound to go wrong. I call it the "oops" factor. It's as cunning as a computer virus and as quick to strike as a bad hair day. Here are a few examples.

 * **Don't forget to check the expiration date on your driver's license (if you plan to drive) and passport well in advance of departure.** When I was younger and better looking . . . okay, when I was younger, I used to travel to Alaska on business. I usually flew roundtrip from Los Angeles to Anchorage, but one time I had the opportunity to take my return flight via Hawaii at no extra charge. What a great deal! Of course, it was the middle of winter in Alaska (think chill factors well below zero), so I had to pack two suitcases, one for each climate. That turned out to be the

least of my worries. I had scheduled rental cars on all four of Hawaii's major islands so that I could drive and photograph each island. While I was in Alaska, however, my trip began to skid off the runway. I found myself with a free afternoon in Anchorage the day before my flight to Hawaii, so I decided to rent a car and go see the Portage Glacier. When I produced my driver's license at the car rental counter, however, I learned to my dismay that it had expired a week ago! I had forgotten to renew it. Technically, the license was still valid for thirty days past its expiration date, but I could tell by the way the agent behind the counter shook her head that I wasn't going to rent a car in Anchorage or Hawaii. Not with that defunct document.

I trudged back to my hotel and sat glumly on the bed staring at my recalcitrant license. How could it betray me like that? My vacation plans were ruined. There was little choice, now, but to change my flight arrangements and return directly to Los Angeles. As the lush, green valleys and sparkling, blue waters of Hawaii began to fade away, I took a closer look at the date on my license and noticed two things. One, the year ended in a zero, and two, the ink on the zero had lost its protective covering. They say desperate people do desperate things, and I can attest to that fact. I had nothing to lose, so I tentatively applied a pencil's eraser to the inner edge of the O and watched in amazement as the ink disappeared. My mind began to spin. If I could change the 0 to a 1, my license would no longer be expired and I would be back in business. I continued to carefully erase the left side of the 0, until only the right side remained. Next, I took the pencil and extended the upper and lower parts of the right side until the number magically became a 1. My drivers license was valid again!

I hurried back to a different car rental agency and, with my tongue stuck somewhere in the back of my mouth, handed over my altered license. I was certain the guilt that warmed my cheeks was broadcasting itself to everyone in the room, but the rental agent never blinked, and in no time at all I was driving to the Portage Glacier.

The following morning I checked out of my hotel and headed

for Hawaii. My success at that rental counter in Anchorage filled me with optimism, and each time I presented my contribution to petty crime at a car rental counter, my confidence grew. I'm happy to report that no one raised so much as an eyebrow, and I was able to drive all four islands as planned. I made darn sure, however, that I never exceeded the speed limit, and I obeyed every law to the letter. Under no circumstances did I want my forgery skills scrutinized by a police officer!

* **Don't ever do what I just told you I did**. I was younger and, if not better looking, definitely more foolish. Anyway, today's drivers licenses are far too sophisticated for my crude effort all those years ago.

* While on the subject of legal and travel documents, **don't grow a beard just before having a new passport photo taken, then shave it off again.** That's exactly what I did prior to leaving for the U.S.S.R. I thought a beard would be dashing, but on me it looked like a briar patch. Removing it was the only solution, but I should have done so *before* having my new passport photo taken, not afterwards. When I arrived at the Moscow airport and handed over my document to the young man in passport control, I sensed immediately that all would not go smoothly. He inspected the bearded picture on my passport, then looked at my clean-shaven face with a frown. After his eyes had scanned my smooth skin for what seemed an eternity, they returned to the briar patch in my photo. The frown deepened, and the process repeated itself not once, but twice. After the third inspection, he gave up and began shuffling papers on his small desk. Others from our flight were streaming through the surrounding passport kiosks with little delay, including Fe who now waited for me by the doors leading to the baggage claim area. I was the only one not moving, and, soon, I was the only one standing at passport control.

Fe shifted her feet nervously, and I started glancing at my watch, certain that every move I made was being observed by hidden cameras. Did I look suspicious? My brow was moist by now, and my temples were throbbing from the tension of standing there alone. At first, I avoided the young man's eyes but quickly

realized that shifty eyes weren't a good sign. I looked up, prepared
to meet his suspicious gaze, but he was no longer looking at me.
His eyes were sweeping the room in search of someone else, and I
realized that he planned to hand me off to a higher authority, which
explained why he'd waited so long. That insight did nothing to
calm my jittery nerves or throbbing temples. Movie scenes reeled
through my head of hapless victims carted off to a Spartan
interrogation room, never to be heard from again.

In the end, all my melodrama was unwarranted. The young
man's superior came over, reviewed my passport, looked me up
and down, and waved me through. What a relief. And I only had
nine years left on my passport. I was already looking forward to
having a new picture taken without the beard.

**\* Don't eat pickled eggplant,** at least not in countries where
the bacteria count in the water is high. (Think Mexico and
Montezuma's revenge.) In my case, we were in Bukhara,
Uzbekistan, where the bacteria count was off the charts. Fe and I
had met four fellow travelers who were on independent itineraries
similar to ours, and we had gotten into the habit of joining one
another for dinner. The group included a young man named Adrian
from Australia, a retired Australian woman who used to be a
doctor, and two Italian women who were friends. Fe and I had
been carefully following the golden rule about eating food in
countries such as Uzbekistan: "If you can't cook it or peel it, don't
eat it." On our first night in Bukhara, however, I let my guard
down and ate pickled egg plant, a dish that was neither cooked nor
peeled. The two Australians made the same mistake, and all three
of us woke up later that night suffering from severely upset
stomachs and diarrhea.

My case was mild enough that I was up and walking the next
day, although not ready to resume sightseeing just yet. The
Australian woman self-medicated and recovered fairly quickly.
Poor Adrian wasn't so lucky. As the day progressed, there was no
sign of improvement, and he seemed to be growing delirious. He'd
been adamant about not being taken to a hospital, but we felt
something had to be done and asked the hotel staff to call a doctor.

A woman arrived to take Adrian's pulse and examine him. When she was done, she turned to me and started gently slapping her face with the palms of her hands. The doctor spoke no English, so it took me a few moments to realize that she wanted my aftershave lotion. I retrieved the bottle from my room, then watched in amazement as she pulled a needle from her bag that was large enough to sedate a horse and old enough to have survived the second world war. I instantly understood the purpose of the aftershave lotion. She intended to sterilize the needle with it! Sure enough, she plunged the needle into the bottle and inserted it into Adrian's arm. Whatever she gave him worked. The next day he was back on his feet and ready to resume his journey. Fe and I were relieved to see how quickly he'd recovered, but we didn't have the nerve to tell him about the needle.

**\* Don't run out of gas just before your cruise ship sails.** Back when sailors navigated by the stars, Fe and I honeymooned in Greece. Okay, I know I'm exaggerating about navigating systems, but it sure *feels* like it was that long ago. The trip was everything we had hoped for and included seven days on a cruise ship visiting the Greek islands. When we reached Rhodes, we joined a couple from the ship for an exciting ride on motorcycles to Lindos, a very picturesque village with a remarkable set of ruins located on the other side of the island. To be honest, the other couple rented a motorcycle. I had never been on anything with two wheels and an engine in my life, so I rented a motorbike, with which I terrorized the local populace while I drove in circles around the public square next to the rental shop trying to learn how to start, stop, and turn corners without tumbling over.

I soon got the hang of it, and off we zoomed with the other couple. Actually, they zoomed. We sort of put-putted. Needless to say, we soon lost sight of them. It was a delightful ride, however, and we arrived in Lindos without incident. It didn't take long to find our friends, and we wandered together around the ruins of an acropolis seated on top of a rocky outcrop, then through the narrow streets of the village below.

The cruise ship was scheduled to depart at 6:00pm, so we

abandoned our idyllic setting by mid-afternoon and headed back across the island. Our friends were soon out of sight, but we weren't worried. All we had to do was stick to the main road and avoid all the crazy drivers. We would be back with plenty of time to spare. Nothing could go wrong . . . go wrong . . .

Until halfway back, when the motorbike ran out of gas! We glided to the side of the road to consider our options. The sun, which had looked so high in the sky just a short while ago, now looked much lower. As I evaluated our situation, I swore I could see it speeding its descent towards the horizon. We couldn't walk back in time, and if we abandoned the motorbike to hitch a ride, there was no telling how much the rental shop would charge us for losing their property. A truck with an empty flat bed would have been ideal, but none presented itself. We had about resigned ourselves to missing our ship's departure when who should appear on the horizon like knights in shining armor but the other couple. They had turned back when they realized no one had told us about the extra gas tank. It turned out that our motorbike had two fuel tanks. All it took was the flip of a switch and we were on the road again. This time, our new friends stayed with us to be sure nothing else went wrong, and we arrived back in Rhodes with time to spare.

 * **Don't ignore the weather in cities where you have connecting flights.** There is nothing more frustrating than failing to reach your final destination on time due to bad weather. At a minimum, there are hotel reservations at stake, and your itinerary may include a tour or cruise ship that you have to chase after. Things can get expensive in a hurry, and a portion of your vacation can be quickly ruined.

For example, the best months for traveling in India are the winter months. The sun shines every day and the temperatures are moderate. However, that's the worst time to fly there, since flights from the U.S. typically require a connecting flight somewhere in Europe where winter storms can wreck havoc with travel plans. Fe and I nearly experienced this dilemma when we flew to Delhi by way of Frankfurt, Germany. Fortunately, we had decided to go a day early so we could get a head start on adapting to the extreme time change, and we had already left Frankfurt when the airport shut down due to a horrific snow storm that swept across all of Europe. People were stranded for days, including two of our fellow travelers who arrived two days later and a third member who never made it at all. Had we not left early . . . well you get the idea. Solution? Consider flying to India by way of Thailand. From California or the west coast, it's about the same time and distance, and it doesn't snow in Thailand! At least not yet.

**\* Don't take long trips to foreign countries with fellow workers or acquaintances you don't know really well.** Traveling in a foreign country is a 24/7 proposition. so I have one word to offer anybody thinking of going with a companion they don't know well: compatibility. You might think you and an officemate (for example) get along quite well, but there are only two sure ways to find out. Either marry them or travel with them. Taking trips to foreign countries is a lot like getting married. The first week, everything's great. You've arrived in an exciting new country, and the world seems fresh and exciting. That's your honeymoon period. Assuming that you don't plan to lie on a beach all day, the second week begins to put a strain on things. You begin to feel the effects of your hectic itinerary, and cracks begin to reveal themselves in your traveling companion. These take the form of idiosyncrasies and quirks you either overlooked or hadn't considered important back home. The toilet paper is too rough. The bed is lumpy. The food tastes funny. One person wants to go to bed; the other wants to stay up and read. One of you takes twice as long as the other to get ready in the morning and is habitually late. By week three, you are ready for a divorce.

The above happened to my wife and I on a trip to Europe. A fellow office worker with whom Fe got along quite well, turned into a whirling dervish of complaints and problems. The trip was hell.

**\* Don't upset the local police and be sure you understand the local customs.** The last thing you want to do is end up in a local jail because you "lost it" for a minute. That happened to three wives who were shopping in a town in Mexico while their husbands attended a business meeting. Two police officers approached the ladies and tried to flirt with them. One of the ladies became quite indignant and said some pretty nasty things. Her anger may have been justified, but that didn't prevent her and her companions from being tossed in jail on a charge of prostitution. A simple bribe before things got out of hand probably would have saved them from their predicament, but hindsight didn't help. The husbands eventually tracked them down, only to learn that the women would have to stay put until a hearing could be arranged with the local judge. They tried a discreet bribe, but it was too late. Once the women had been booked, there was little they could do. There was, however, another option. The husbands were told that prostitution was perfectly legal in that country, as long as the prostitutes were registered. All it took to get their wives released was a quick trip to city hall where they paid a fee (think bribe) to have their loved ones officially registered as prostitutes! Imagine the stories the husbands must have told when they got back home.

Which reminds me of *my* first business trip to Mexico City, and the warning I was given from a work mate about the country's unusual laws regarding taxis. I was told to never put my luggage in the trunk of a cab. Keep it next to me in the back seat, instead. Why? According to my mentor, when I hailed a cab in Mexico, I became responsible for my driver and what he did behind the wheel. If he got in an accident, I was held accountable because I had hired him. In the case of a bad accident, I could be thrown in jail. If it was only a fender bender, a bribe would probably suffice, but my co-worker's advice was "don't stick around to find out about damages. Grab your suitcase, jump out of the cab, and run!"

Fortunately, I never had to put his advice to the test, but after sitting in a few back seats, I held my luggage closely and prayed a lot. Cab drivers, all Mexican drivers for that matter, thought they were matadors and the streets were one large bullring. It was not uncommon for my driver to suddenly decide to shoot across three lanes of heavy traffic without so much as a backward glance. A quick look in the rearview mirror was all he needed, and off we went! My initial reaction was something akin to an animal caught in the clutches of a wild predator: panic followed by surrender. I never did get used to such wild antics, but I quickly learned to never look back.

**\* Don't arrive in Venice, Italy, without knowing precisely where your hotel is located.** The porters will eat you alive. Getting to the island of Venice is generally accomplished by taking a train from the mainland to the Santa Lucia Station. From there you face several choices. 1) You can drag your suitcases through a maze of alleyways in hopes that you will find the Piazza San Marco or other notable landmark before the sun sets. 2) You can cram your luggage onto a crowded vaporetto and take the equivalent of a local bus ride up the Grand Canal to the appropriate vaporetto station, where you will, once again, find yourself in a maze of narrow streets once you've disembarked. 3) You can hire a motor coach to whisk you up the Grand Canal in style to the appropriate landing area, where you may still face those blasted little streets and have paid three times as much for the privilege. 4) You can hire a porter.

Porters come in a variety of shapes and sizes, but they all have one goal in common: to shift as many euros as possible from your pockets to their pockets. There are no fixed rates for hiring a porter. What you pay will depend on what you think is fair and how determined you are not to be bullied out of a week's pay. The porter will complain loudly about how far your hotel is from the station and how many pieces of luggage you have; he will lead you down side streets that extend your route and justify a bigger tip; and he will never be satisfied with the money you offer him when you eventually reach your hotel.

Case in point. On one of our trips to Venice, Fe and I were disembarking from a cruise ship instead of the train. The cruise ships dock at locations a lot closer to the Piazza San Marcos than the train station, but that doesn't mean your fees to reach your hotel are going to be any cheaper. In our case, porters were standing at the ready to take ours and the other passengers' suitcases to our hotels, or so we thought. Instead, they took us about 200 yards along the waterfront to a small canal where they handed us over to those expensive motor coaches I mentioned earlier. I pulled out the equivalent of five dollars in Euros and tried to hand it to my porter, only to have him refuse it. He slammed his right fist into his left palm and demanded more. I figured five dollars was a pretty good tip in any country for such a short distance and decided to stand my ground. I held out the money again, and let him know if he didn't want it, I would keep it. After a few more theatrics, he grabbed the bills from my hand and stalked off in a huff. I chuckled at his antics, but I could see that reaching our hotel was no laughing matter. I'd been to Venice twice before, and I had a pretty good idea what was going to happen. The expensive motor coaches would take us about two more blocks to the Piazza, and we would be handed off to another army of porters who would finally take us to our hotels. Follow that script, and we were going to be fleeced good and proper. So, I placed our suitcases against the wall of the nearest building and asked Fe to guard them while I went in search of our hotel. It turned out that our lodgings were less than two blocks away down one of those narrow streets. We followed the directions that I had been given and found the place with no problem. Once we had checked in, we walked to the Piazza in time to see the last of the ship's passengers following their porters across the square. They looked totally helpless, and I couldn't help feeling a bit sorry for them. How much more did they pay, I wondered, to reach their hotels? I'm betting at least another $30 each.

That incident with the porter, by the way, is described in the first chapter of one of my novels, *Venice Lost*.

# CHAPTER EIGHT
*If I Am What I Eat, Who Am I??*

"Vegetables aren't food. Vegetables are what food eats!"

I'll never forget this delightful quote. It came from a fellow traveler who was consuming a generous portion of meat during dinner on an African safari Fe and I were taking from the Masai Mara in Kenya to the Serengeti plains in Tanzania. It was early July and the famous wildebeest migration was underway. Thousands of those bizarre looking beasts (imagine an animal shaped something like a buffalo, with a flat, elongated face that might have been painted by Modigliani, a shaggy head badly in need of a haircut, and curved horns) trek north from Tanzania that time of year and cross the Mara River into Kenya in search of greener, summer pastures. They are joined by zebras which help keep a lookout for predators, such as lions and hyenas trailing the massive herds and wait for weaker prey to fall behind. The weaker animals become easy pickings for the meat eaters. As we watched the carcass of a wildebeest being consumed by lions, I couldn't help thinking about our traveling companion and his declaration about food. Could he be part predator, I wondered?

There are three topics that are often raised when we travel. These are the weather (which we've already discussed), regularity (which we will not discuss), and food. Food often comes up as a topic of conversation when we have returned from a trip somewhere outside the U.S. People always seem fascinated by what we ate. This can cause me some embarrassment, because half the time I can't remember. I love to eat, and I remember whether the food was particularly good, but I have a devil of a time describing precisely what the food was or how it was prepared. It took me awhile to figure out why I have this blank spot in my memory, but I believe I have the answer.

Other than nuking things in the micro-wave or firing up the barbeque, I don't know how to cook, and I have little desire to learn. I blame this deficiency on a traumatic event that I experienced in my young, adult life. When I graduated from college, the only apartment I could afford looked like it had been built during the Great Depression, but that was okay. I had my first job, and I was on my own. So, there I was, my first night in my very own living space, trying to cook spaghetti. While I prepared the noodles, I turned on the oven, which looked even older than the apartment building, to warm some garlic bread. "Turning on the oven" consisted of turning on a gas burner and lighting a match to a flash tube located inside the oven. In theory, the flame flashed down the tube and lit the oven burner. In reality, so many match heads had fallen into the flash tube over the years, it had become impossible for the flame to reach the burner. Instead, the little blue flame sat at the mouth to the tube and waited. I didn't know this and put the bread in the oven and closed the door.

As I drained the spaghetti, gas fumes were building inside the oven until they reached ignition stage. At that point, the oven door blew open and shut again with a BLAM-BLAM that nearly gave me a heart attack. I threw up my hands in alarm and scattered spaghetti all over the ceiling. Heart racing, I opened the oven and discovered that the burner was now lighted and the bread was warming. I scrapped the spaghetti off the ceiling and proceeded with dinner.

After that, whenever I wanted to use the oven, I would simply light the flash tube and wait in the living room until the oven door went BLAM-BLAM. Fortunately, I was soon able to afford a better apartment and moved out before I blew up the entire building. I've never talked to a psychiatrist about that episode, but you can see how it could affect my subconscious when it comes to cooking. It didn't affect my desire to eat, however. I'm really good at that.

One of my earliest travel adventures took me to Japan. That would have been in the late 1960s. I had never eaten sushi, but I had heard about sushi bars and couldn't wait to try one. The thought of eating raw fish only heightened my sense of adventure. My first night in Tokyo, I went to the hotel concierge and told him I wanted to have dinner at an authentic sushi bar. He wrote the name of a restaurant on the back of a hotel card and told me to show it to any cab driver. He also told me not to lose the card, which was in Japanese, because none of the cab drivers spoke English. I would need the card to return to the hotel.

I hopped into a cab, showed the driver the address on the card, and off we went. It was raining that night, and all the windows in the cab had fogged up. Two things immediately caught my attention. First, my driver sped through the streets like the proverbial bat out of hell, and second, he could hardly see a thing. He kept wiping a small spot on the windshield to see if he was about to hit anything and another on the driver-side window so he could see his rear view mirror. Oh yes, there was one more thing. He drove without headlights. We might as well have been driving through wet laundry. The only positive note: there wasn't much traffic.

We rocketed into the heart of the city and soon were scooting up and down back streets in the Ginza district while my driver tried to find the restaurant. I learned later that it was common in those days for addresses to be shown on maps located every few blocks or so. There were no street numbers on the buildings themselves.

You had to read the map, then count the number of dwellings on the correct street to find the one you were looking for. I don't know if that was the problem that night. All I knew was that we were entering some very dark streets, and the words abducted and kidnapped were swirling through my mind.

No sooner had I begun to fret than we rounded a corner, and I saw a brightly lighted sign announcing my sushi bar. I tipped the driver handsomely for delivering me there alive and approached the establishment. A cacophony of voices greeted me when I opened the front door, followed by silence. Remember all those western movies where a stranger with two six shooters enters the bar, and everybody grows quiet and turns to stare? That's how I felt, but without the stares. The place was filled with Japanese families sitting on pillows around tables with chopsticks in their hands, but they were too polite to look directly at me. They peeked at me out of the corners of their eyes, instead.

I had asked the hotel concierge for an authentic sushi bar, and authentic was what I got. There wasn't a "foreign" face in the place. My attention was immediately drawn to the far side of the room where three men in white aprons stood behind a counter busily chopping up dead fish and calling out finished orders to the waitresses. It goes without saying that the place smelled of fish. The setting was exactly as I'd imagined it, and when a hostess approached, I nodded towards the counter.

She seated me on a stool in front of a highly polished countertop behind which sat three glass cases filled with every imaginable kind of underwater creature. How fresh was the food, I wondered. In answer, a long, spindly thing that reminded me of a giant grasshopper rolled over on its bed of ice! The food was definitely fresh. The room hummed with voices as the diners returned to their meals. The chefs continued to bark out commands to the servers, and chopsticks clicked nosily against bowls. The clatter and voices made me feel that I had been accepted somehow, and the tension I had felt upon entering slid away.

A smiling waitress handed me a small menu, but I shook my head to indicate I couldn't read it. I pointed to the glass cases and said "sushi," then tipped my hand to my mouth and said "sake." She nodded knowingly and spoke in rapid-fire Japanese to one of the men behind the counter. Before I knew it, the chef began plopping chopped up food items on one of the glass cases in front of me. Someone, I can't remember who, once told me that sushi bars were kept so clean, you could eat off the counters, so I picked up something that looked like seaweed and placed it on the counter in front of me. The room instantly filled with giggles, but when I swung my head around, everyone was bent over their bowls and plates, furiously working their chopsticks. I had expected to find a sea of faces watching me, but not one eye caught mine. The Japanese were simply too polite to be caught staring. They were, however, observing my every move. My face reddened as I realized I'd committed a *faux pas*. How, I wondered, did you say *that* in Japanese? The waitress hurried over with my sake and placed a wooden stand shaped like a miniature footstool on the counter. I quickly put my food on it and started eating. In addition to the seaweed, I was given generous portions of various raw fish. I had no idea what I was eating, and I quickly ordered more sake to fortify my nerves and stomach.

The cab ride back to the hotel was just as exciting as the ride to the Ginza District, but after all that sake I no longer worried.

Earlier, I shared some exciting stories about traveling in the Soviet Union, but I never mentioned the menus. Fe and I were traveling alone, so we were on our own for meals, and that was perfectly okay with us. Venturing out to unfamiliar restaurants to order unfamiliar food items in unfamiliar countries was part of the travel adventure. This particular journey started in Tbilisi, Georgia, where we wandered the streets in search of our first meal as dusk settled over the city. We soon came upon a quaint, old restaurant with tiled floors, high ceilings, varnished tables, and padded chairs. The setting looked perfect, and we entered. The waiter who greeted us spoke little English, but he seated us with a flourish and handed us beautifully bound menus with pages of parchment-style paper. The menus looked old enough to be part of the Dead Sea Scrolls, and we poured over the beautifully scripted pages at great length while the waiter disappeared into the kitchen. We had no idea what to order, but our stomachs were growling loudly enough to let the world know that we were ready to eat. But where was our waiter?

Twenty minutes passed before he revealed himself, and we eagerly started pointing to items we thought might be interesting to try. The waiter responded with a firm "nyet" and directed us to the back page where three selections had been penciled in at the bottom. It turned out that those were the only food choices available. We had just spent twenty minutes perusing menus beautiful enough to hang in the Louvre, only to discover that we couldn't order anything except one of those three items. Similar experiences followed at other restaurants as we traveled around the Soviet Union, and we quickly learned to ignore the elaborate pages filled with nonexistent food dishes and turn to the last page for the "meal du jour."

While the food selections in the old Soviet Union may not have been so great, at least we could eat at a civilized hour, say six o'clock. In Brazil and other Latin American countries, people didn't even think about dinner before eight or nine. Try as we might, we couldn't adapt to this local custom. Most of the restaurants opened around 7:00pm. By then, we were already hungry, but we tried to hold out awhile for appearances sake. By seven-thirty, however, we were too famished to wait any longer and hurried to the nearest restaurant, where we invariably found ourselves surrounded by empty tables and bored waiters who looked at us like we were crazy.

Some of our more exciting meals were eaten in Brazil. There, they had restaurants called churrascarias, which were famous for their tasty, barbecued meats. The waiters didn't act bored in those establishments. Nor did they hide in the kitchen for half-an- hour. Once we were seated, all we had to do was turn over the markers on our table. One side of the marker was red and the other green. The green side read Sim Por Favor and when it was turned up, it signaled to the waiters that we were ready to eat. A parade of waiters suddenly descended on us with every type of meat imaginable. Each waiter sliced a hearty portion of his specialty and put it on our plates. He was followed by another waiter, and another, until our plates were piled high with beef, pork, ham, and who knew what else. The only way to stop this parade of carnage was to turn over our markers to the red side which read Nao Obrigado. Instantly, the waiters stopped coming, and we could wade through our mounds of food. Meanwhile, the waiters were busily descending upon other tables.

I mentioned earlier that I have a hard time remembering precisely what I have eaten on these ventures around the world. I guess what matters most to me is not only what I ate, but where and how. How memorable was each meal? It might be a cultural experience, such as the churrascarias restaurants I just described, a particular waiter, or a special setting.

One of the most memorable meals Fe and I ever had took place in Tibet during our overland journey from Kathmandu to Lhasa. The main towns of Shegar, Shigatse, and Gyantse had Chinese restaurants that catered to foreigners, but it took a full day to travel from one town to the next, and the only other restaurants found along the way were local establishments in tiny villages that fed the Tibetans. One look at their kitchens was all you needed to decide that you didn't want to eat there. They consisted of dirt floors and stone walls covered with so much black soot it was hard to see the original surface. The cook stove was a block of concrete with an opening at the bottom for firewood and a couple of holes in the top where greasy pans sat over open flames. Empty beer bottles and discarded cartons were scattered about the room. Dogs wandered in and were shooed out. The restaurants themselves usually consisted of a few battle-scared, wooden tables and chairs that looked like refugees from some third world conflict.

So, when the driver stopped each day at a small village, he and the guide disappeared into one of those local establishments for lunch while we stayed in the van and munched on bags of trail mix and other snacks. It wasn't a bad routine, and it gave us a chance to stretch our legs and explore a bit after we had eaten.

At one village, however, our noonday break turned into something akin to an out-of-body experience. We had pulled out our snacks as usual, but no sooner had our guide and driver disappeared than the van was surrounded by a dozen Tibetans. At first, we thought they wanted to sell us souvenirs, but all they did was press their faces against the windows and stare at us. After several minutes, they changed windows much like a game of musical chairs. Were they begging for food? That explanation was certainly plausible, but the Tibetans we had met on our journey seemed to have enough to eat. Trying to share our snacks was out of the question. We knew if we opened the door or windows, we would be swarmed by these onlookers, and we had to make our limited supply of food items last us three more days. We decided it was best to ignore them. So there we sat, guiltily munching our snacks and trying to ignore the noses flattened against the windowpanes.

We assumed the Tibetans would leave once we had finished our brief meal, but they continued their silent game of musical chairs long after we had put our food away and only dispersed when they knew our guide was about to return. What had they wanted? Not that many tourists took the overland route, so it was possible we were a simply a novelty to them, and they were curious to look at us. We asked our guide about the incident, but he was clearly uncomfortable and had little to say on the matter. One thing I did know: that was one meal I would never forget. Mark it down as memorable.

One of my fondest dining memories took place at a hotel in Pontorson, France. Why was I in Pontorson? Because the town was near Mont-St.-Michel, a great rock that Mother Nature had thrust into the air like a giant fist along the western coast of France. It wasn't just the rock that made the place so special. It was the flat expanse of sand that surrounded the rock and stretched for several miles towards the horizon, where the English Channel lurked just out of sight. During high tides, ocean water flooded the landscape and surrounded the rock.

As I approached Mont-St.-Michel, I noted an abbey adorned with stone cloisters and secluded sanctuaries sitting majestically atop this rocky throne as if observing its realm. Below, a tiny village of tourist shops wound its way up the lower portion of the rock, and three wooden fishing boats lay on their sides in the sand. The boats looked clumsy and helpless. They reminded me of beached whales waiting for the tide to rescue them, and when I saw two fishermen approaching, I suspected they would soon be set free.

I turned my gaze to the horizon in time to see the sand begin to shimmer with the seductive dance of a desert mirage. Was it my imagination, or was there now a hint of blue water where land met sky? My question was soon answered as fingers of water slithered across the porous surface towards me. The mirage had been transformed into a blue veil, its leading edge hissing as the sand tried in vain to absorb the advancing tide that marched relentlessly towards the shore. It reminded me of an alien creature in a horror movie that would not be stopped. At first, the water could be measured in inches, then feet. It wasn't long before I had to retreat to the causeway that connected Mont-St.-Michel to the mainland. Water surrounded me; the fishermen's boats had been joyfully released from their sandy bonds; and the massive rock known as Mont-St.-Michel had become an island.

The unfolding drama helped me work up an excellent appetite, and I returned to my hotel in anticipation of a fine dinner. There was a small problem, however. I had taken a few French courses in school, but the words I'd learned for different kinds of food -- *poisson* for fish, *poulet* for chicken, *beouf* for beef, *legume* for vegetable -- did not appear on French menus. Nothing looked familiar, with the result that I rarely got what I thought I was ordering. A plate of ham turned out to be a pork sandwich, and so forth. It was the same everywhere I went in France, and by the time I arrived in Pontorson, I was quite wary of French menus.

I had taken most of my meals at my hotel and always had the same waiter. He was a young man who seemed determined to become the finest waiter in France, if not all of Europe. His service and attention to details were impeccable, right down to the towel he hung with such precision over his left forearm, and the way he smartly kicked open the swinging doors leading to the kitchen when he left the room carrying a tray of dishes balanced on his right hand above his head.

This would be my last dinner at the hotel, and I opened the menu with as much hope as temerity. My eyes were instantly drawn to the dinner special, which I was certain translated into duck l'orange, one of my favorite dishes. After so many disappointments, however, I didn't want to take any chances, so I tried in my faltering French to confirm this translation with my young waiter. He couldn't speak a word of English and had no idea what I was saying, but he was so determined to understand me, his smile morphed into a grimace and sweat broke out on his brow. The tension in his face was palpable, and I could see that my line of questioning was going nowhere. In desperation, I tucked my hands under my armpits, looked up at my waiter, and flapped my elbows up and down in a flying motion. Then I quacked at him. The busy dining room became noticeably quieter; many eyes turned to stare. Mostly French eyes, I might add. I knew what they were thinking. There's another one of those strange American tourists making a fool of himself. I had to admit that they were right. I mean, how would you react if you saw someone holding his armpits and flapping his elbows while quacking like a duck?

The effect on my waiter, however, could only be described as therapeutic. The tension lines fled from his face, and his grimace returned to a smile. Vigorously, he nodded his head up and down to signify a "oui." I may have set back French impressions of Americans for another fifty years, but by gosh I got my duck l'orange!

As I said before, it isn't so much the food as the experience that is memorable to me. That's what made that last dinner in Pontorson so special. The look on my waiter's face when I quacked was priceless. Here are a few more special moments.

The Dolomites in northern Italy offer a theatrical setting of jagged mountain peaks that jut abruptly out of the verdant hills near the Austrian border. Fe and I followed winding roads on a sun-drenched day through a series of secluded valleys and past alpine villages, all surrounded by towering, granite mountains. The area was famous for its ski resorts in winter, and during the summer and fall, it offered vistas right out of the movie Sound of Music. It was late in the season when we were there, but the weather looked promising, and we packed some food in anticipation of a great outing. We had gotten a late start that day, and it was late-afternoon by the time we came upon a meadow surrounded rocky spirals and stopped to eat. We spread our blanket and enjoyed a period of great peace and solitude while we munched on our sandwiches and sipped our wine. As time passed, a remarkable transformation took place. The lowering sun changed the color palettes around us; the granite walls shifted from black and grey to brilliant hues of red, pink, and orange. We were surrounded by such vivid colors, it was like eating in an art museum painted by nature. I have no memory of what was in the sandwiches that day, but I will never forget the setting.

A few weeks later, we returned to the Dolomites and discovered that winter had arrived. Those summer scenes we had enjoyed so much had been put away and replaced by wintry landscapes covered in snow. Almost overnight, the tourists had vanished, and the inns and chalets had closed for a brief respite before the beginning of ski season. We found a chalet that was still open and decided to stay the night. The next morning, I rose at dawn and drove into the Dolomites to catch the sunrise, and what a sunrise it was! This time the transformation went from grey granite to shimmering copper and gold rock walls beautifully draped in a mantle of white snow. I was only munching on a pastry while I photographed that exquisite light show, but I still counted it as a memorable meal, my second in the Dolomites.

According to my criteria, Venice is one big memorable meal. It's virtually impossible to find a place to eat there that isn't located in a great setting along one of the city's many canals. There was one restaurant, however, that was memorable because it wasn't situated along a canal. It was called the Madonna, and it was tucked away down one of the narrow side streets near the Rialto Bridge. The place bustled with locals, most of whom were sitting around large tables covered with plastic table cloths, drinking coffees and liquors, and smoking volumes of cigarettes. The host who greeted us had one of those bowling ball bellies, and face to match, that attested to the many fine meals of pasta he'd eaten there. The great rooms were filled with boisterous Italian voices, and the food was plentiful, tasty, and reasonably priced, a rare find in Venice. What the restaurant lacked was tourists. It gave the place an authentic air that couldn't be duplicated among the popular restaurants along the Grand Canal, and it made us feel as if we had time-traveled back to another century. (In fact, I describe the restaurant in my novel, Venice Lost, which does involve time travel in Venice.) Fe and I had more than one memorable meal there, dining with the locals.

Years ago in the Philippines, I enjoyed a great lunch at the Villa Escadero Ranch, located a couple hours drive from Manila. The dining area consisted of picnic-style tables and benches that sat in about two feet of water. You had to remove shoes and socks and roll up pant legs before wading to the tables. Why do it? Like other Southeast Asian countries, the Philippines had enough heat and humidity to create its own version of global warming, so dangling your feet in the water while eating lumpia and other Filipino delicacies was an invigorating treat. There was also a waterfall nearby that circulated the cool water and produced a refreshing mist. After lunch, I wandered about the grounds where I found men tilling the fields with plows pulled by water buffalo and the women harvesting green rice stalks from flooded paddies. There was even a show featuring Filipino dances and music. All in all, it was a great way to spend a day, and definitely a memorable meal.

If you ever get to Manila, I would recommend giving the Villa Escadero Ranch a try. However, my visit to the ranch was twenty-five years ago, so things may have changed!

# CHAPTER NINE
*Culture Means People Unlike Us*

Amasya has some of the finest wooden Ottoman houses remaining in Turkey, but the highlight of my visit there was the four school girls I met that day. As usual, I had risen at dawn to photograph the city's best features in the early morning light. I wandered through the timeworn streets capturing many tantalizing images, from the bizarre (five pairs of bright red, long john undergarments hanging from a clothing line) to the steadfast (a grey haired lady bent halfway to the ground under the weight of a bag of rice she carried home on her back). There was one wooden house in particular that I knew could make an excellent composition, but the lighting wasn't right and it lacked a focal point. It needed the right subject matter, and I filed it away in my memory bank for future reference.

Later that morning, I chanced upon the four, charming, teenage school girls that I mentioned before. They bounced up to me in their white blouses and blue skirts with a flurry of energy and asked me to take their picture. I immediately thought of the house I had noted earlier. It happened to be nearby, so I motioned for them to follow me. They literally danced down the street around me, chatting and laughing all the way. Once I had them lined up in front of the house, I motioned for them to jump up and down. They happily complied, and the result was a striking picture of the four of them with their feet off the ground, their hair flying, and their faces lit up by giant grins.

The best was yet to come, however. They now grabbed my hands and motioned for me to follow *them*. Less than two blocks away, they showed me a side street where a group of smaller girls, perhaps eight or nine years old, were seated along the curb in festive costumes that included white scarves with floral designs, caps embroidered with small coins, and yellow parkas. They looked like a swarm of bees that had landed beside the road. I sat down opposite them and captured a series of remarkable close ups with my telephoto lens.

My experience in Amasya raises an interesting question. What is the difference between human encounters, like the lady of the opera, and culture? It's often difficult to distinguish between the two, because they both involve people. When I think of people, I think of those four school girls in Amasya. Their spontaneous behavior and vibrant personalities made them literally leap out from the crowd. They were memorable, but I'm not sure their behavior reflected Turkish society as a whole, which is how I define culture. On the other hand, the smaller girls in their costumes were obviously preparing for an event that had strong cultural overtones.

Here's another example. In the Lady of the Opera chapter I described the two peasant women in Yugoslavia who wanted me to take their picture. That was a great memory of people. A few miles away, I came upon a husband and wife hitching up an old, wooden plow to a horse. When I got out of the car with my camera, the man saw me and posed proudly behind the plow while his wife held the reins to guide the horse. It made a nice composition, but after I had taken the shot and they thought I was finished, the two switched places. It was the man who held the reins and the woman who did the heavy lifting behind the plow! Farther along, I discovered four women in a small field bent over and tilling the earth with hand trowels while a man stood in front of them leaning on a shovel. It didn't take long for me to figure out that it was the women who did the real labor. The men merely supervised. Those two incidents were examples of culture.

Gender can play an interesting role in culture. In Tibet, I came across two women dressed in colorful layers of clothing who were taking a brief break from their labors in a small dye factory. Their pose leaning against the doorframe to the factory was lovely, but before I could take their picture, they went back inside. The Tibetans were very warm and friendly people, and I'd had little difficulty photographing them. So I followed the women inside in hopes that I could encourage them to return to the doorway and pose for me. It was a poorly lit room with a toxic odor that pinched my nose and made my eyes water, and I was sure they would be happy to escape again for a brief respite. But when I tried to coax them back outside, they simply smiled and ignored my request. I was about to give up when Fe stepped forward and urged them to "come on" with a wave of her hand. To my surprise, they readily agreed and returned to their position in the doorway. That picture has always been one of my favorites, and I learned a lesson that helped during the rest of the trip. The Tibetan women were very independent and did not always do what men wanted. After the incident at the dye factory, I let Fe intercede for me with the women.

Earlier, I described my adventure at that sushi bar in the Ginza District in Tokyo. That certainly qualified as a cultural experience. In fact, I would call it a cultural shock! The Asian countries I have visited were filled with cultural surprises, and Japan was no exception. There are too many examples to remember them all here. They seemed to happen about every ten feet. One that stands out took place in Kyoto. Each morning, elderly women swept the streets and temple grounds with bristle hand brooms that required them to stoop over while they patiently gathered up leaves and other loose debris in woven baskets. It was back-bending work, and they weren't even paid for their efforts. Why did they do it? Because they felt it was their duty.

On a lighter note, everywhere I went in Japan I saw Japanese groups posing for photographs. Picture taking was popular. Rain or shine, it didn't matter. They lined up in rows in front of every temple and statue, and when it rained, they all popped open their umbrellas and posed anyway. I often stepped behind the photographer and took a similar picture. The group shots added an interesting dimension to my photographs of Japan.

Anytime you travel to a foreign country you're going to encounter new cultures that define the way people live. That's part of the fun of traveling abroad. It also helps us define our own travel experiences. Some of those experiences can be particularly personal and memorable. Here are a few of my favorites.

During a trip to the Peruvian portion of the Amazon basin, Fe and I hiked through the rain forest to a clearing dominated by a thatched community lodge that at one time had housed several Yagua Indian families in a single, cavernous room. They no longer lived there, but they returned at regular intervals to meet with tourists like us. They had no use for money, so we traded with them. We offered t-shirts, tennis shoes, kitchen utensils, and other practical items in exchange for necklaces, baskets, and masks, all made by hand from materials that were indigenous to the Amazon region. The leader of the small tribe proudly wore a large, plastic bib with a lobster printed on it that he had previously received in trade. It was apparent from his beaming face that he considered it a prized possession. Everyone in the tribe wore thatched skirts and little else. The children were forbidden candy because their teeth had little resistance to sugar and were very susceptible to cavities. Naturally, that was the first thing for which they asked when their parents weren't looking. The village scene was packed with cultural images: a grandmother searching through her young charge's hair for lice; men demonstrating their accuracy with blow guns; a woman stringing bits of bone and dried berries to make a necklace.

It seemed an idyllic life, yet most of the young adults were missing. We learned they had gone to Iquitos to find work. The modern world was encroaching on their way of life, and it was no longer possible to sustain themselves by living off the land. Thanks to their trade with tourists, they were able to retain some of their traditions, but for how much longer? I feared it wouldn't be too many years before the Yagua culture disappeared completely.

Some cultures remain frozen in time. There can be many reasons for this, but in Burma (now called Myanmar) the reason is politics. Burma was a very poor country when I was there twenty-five years ago, and it has seen little change since then. That's because the country has been held in the brutal grip of a military junta that has kept its borders closed to outside influences. Religion is everybody's salvation. The Burmese are devout Buddhists. Each morning I saw young monks walking through the villages barefoot or in sandals, collecting small tokens of money and handfuls of rice to sustain them and their temples for another day. A significant portion of the population was monks.

When I think about Burma, memories flood over me as irresistibly as that tide at Mont St. Michel. The guide of our little tour group was a young mother who couldn't breast feed her baby because she had to work. She needed powdered milk to feed her newborn, but that was out of reach. Powdered milk was sold only in stores for foreigners. So, rather than give her tips, she asked us to buy powdered milk for her baby.

When we reached Mandalay, we saw the famous Irawaddy River whose breadth and length made me think of the Mississippi River, but the comparison ended there. Instead of boats and ships carrying commerce up and down the river, I watched men towing barges with long ropes. The barges were filled with goods and people who could afford to pay for the trip. The men walked along footpaths by the shore and literally hauled the barges up the river by hand. The laborers' work was no different than that of a mule or horse, neither of which they could afford.

Some people didn't have enough money to put a roof over their heads, and they had to find shelter wherever they could, including in the many temples scattered throughout the country. It was not unusual to discover one or more families cooking food over a small fire on the grounds of a temple while barefooted children raced through the elegantly carved archways and corridors.

Our final stop took us to Inle Lake. On the way, we spotted a tiny village comprised of three houses built on stilts, and we urged our guide to stop. Our arrival created quite a stir, and the families quickly gathered to greet us. We were probably as much of a novelty to them as they were to us. My favorite memory was of a woman washing clothes in the tiny stream that ran past the houses. She was crouched down on a log spanning the water and smoking a cheroot while she scrubbed a soapy fabric with her hands. Cheroot smoking was a common sight among Burmese women. I often saw them enjoying their tobacco on the temple grounds or in the open markets where they sold the handfuls of vegetables they had grown.

Inle Lake was a vast body of water where people lived in stilt houses similar to the ones in the tiny village where we had just stopped. They grew crops wherever they could along the water's edge. Some even grew crops, such as tomatoes, on the lake itself in the form of floating gardens. When the wind was calm, the lake became a mirror that reflected the billowing clouds and jade green mountains ringing it. This created the perfect backdrop to one of the cultural highlights of the trip -- watching the butterfly fishermen ply their trade. They stood in the back of narrow boats and propelled themselves along by pushing a vertical oar with their foot in a quick, circular motion. The oar was attached to the back of the boat and worked much like the oar of a Venetian gondola, only these men used their feet instead of their hands. Their odd name, butterfly fishermen, was derived from the way they caught their fish. When they spotted a fish, they plunged a bamboo cage shaped like a butterfly net into the water and scooped their catch onboard.

Throughout Asia, many women used umbrellas to protect themselves from the sun. This was particularly prevalent in the warmer climates, such as Malaysia, Indonesia, and the Philippines, where the women were often seen walking along in the shade of their colorful parasols. Why the umbrellas? Because of their culture. In many Asian societies, women with lighter skin are considered more attractive than those who are darker. So women try to avoid direct sunlight as much as possible to enhance their beauty.

Such behavior is in direct contrast to many western cultures where sun worshippers bask in the hot sunshine in search of the perfect tan. In those countries, darker is better, and in some parts of the world, women even sunbathe topless to avoid a tan line. In Budapest, Hungary, for example, Fe and I often saw women lying bare breasted on towels spread out on flat rocks beneath the bridge leading to Magarite Island. Boy did that look uncomfortable! Topless bathing was also a common sight on the French Riviera, where sun enthusiasts paid outlandish hotel prices so they could lie on a beach of stones and pebbles. For those prices don't you think the tourist bureau could afford to import a little sand?

Now western behavior is changing, thanks to the thinning ozone layer. Suntan lotions are being replaced by sun block as sun lovers around the world adapt to the threat of those dangerous ultraviolet rays. Darker is no longer so beautiful, and our culture is looking a lot more like the Asians'. We may soon be walking around with our own parasols on sunny days.

One of the most wholesome cultural events I have seen took place over twenty-five years ago in Xian, China, which was already becoming famous for its life-sized terracotta soldiers, horses and chariots. The terracotta figures had been discovered by a farmer when he uncovered pottery buried in the ground while digging a water well. Archeologists soon arrived and began to excavate the site. Thousands of figures emerged from the farmer's soil, all created by skilled craftsmen some 2,200 years ago to accompany and protect the first emperor of the Qin Dynastery, Emperor Qin Shi Huang, on his journey after death. It is estimated that artisans toiled for thirty-six years to create the vast army that accompanied the emperor to his grave. Now the army stood before me in somber rows, still waiting for their marching orders.

Those terracotta warriors were the reason I had come to Xian, but the cultural event I mentioned occurred while I wandered through the city's streets. This was in the 1980s, and while the terracotta figures had generated a lot of interest, not that many tourists had yet visited the site. Local customs had hardly changed over the years. So there I was, standing on a street corner watching butchers chopping meat with cleavers in the beds of old, wooden wagons when two women began shouting to the workers around them. A crowd quickly gathered, and a group of about fifty people stepped forward and lined up at either end of a sturdy rope that had been stretched along the street. The opposing sides each grabbed the rope and began an old fashioned tug-of-war while the spectators roared their approval. The struggle lasted for several minutes until one side was pulled across the center line and accepted their defeat. It was all good-natured fun with onlookers congratulating the losers as well as the winners. The crowd soon disbursed and returned to the butchers and other food merchants to buy produce for their evening meals.

I can't leave Xian without sharing a funny side story. It had to do with my hotel, a brand new building that would have made any five-star property proud. Except it was run more like a three-star pension. The Chinese had not yet gotten the hang of providing outstanding service. It wasn't for lack of trying. For example, when my client and I visited Guilin, we went to a restaurant in another brand new hotel that bragged about its authentic American cuisine. We had been eating Chinese food for over a week by then, and while the food was always delicious, our mouths were watering for an old fashioned hamburger with fries or medium-rare steak. So we hurried to the new restaurant at dinnertime and waited expectantly for the bottle of cabernet sauvignon wine and the chateaubriand steaks we had just ordered. The steak eventually arrived, but not the wine. When we asked our waiter about it, he nodded nervously and told us in broken English that it would come soon. Puzzled, we began to eat, only to discover that any connection between the meat in front of us and chateaubriand was due entirely to our hungry imaginations. We couldn't help but chuckle at the cooks' valiant efforts to produce western-style cuisine and ate our meals without complaint. But where was that stupid bottle of wine? It finally arrived just as we were about to order desert. Where, we wanted to know, had it been? The waiter looked at us with sheepish eyes and admitted that the hotel had only one bottle opener, and no one could find it. Somehow, they had finally removed the cork, and our waiter now filled our glasses with a great flourish. After such a Herculean effort, we could hardly send the bottle back. So we drank the wine with our desert, which consisted of something they called baked Alaska but which tasted more like burnt Mongolia.

But I have digressed. Back to that hotel in Xian. Our schedule required us to rise before dawn the next morning, eat our breakfast, and leave for the airport before sunup. Our alarms woke us on schedule, and we quickly prepared to leave. When we vacated our rooms, however, we plunged into total darkness. The lights worked in our rooms, but that was it. The frugal, hotel staff had turned off all the lights in the hallways and lobbies to save electricity. Leaving our rooms was like stepping from broad daylight into a cavern filled with bats. We never knew if our next step would send us crashing into a table or tumbling down a flight of stairs. All we could do was hug the nearest wall and feel our way along in the general direction of the hotel lobby. At last, we spotted a feeble, yellow light across a courtyard and made a beeline for it on the theory that where there was light, there was breakfast. Our theory proved correct, and I'm happy to report that we found the restaurant without killing ourselves or disturbing any bats.

One of the most time-honored traditions in many parts of the world is bargaining. It is done with great relish, current company excluded. Let's face it, many Europeans and Americans don't really know how to bargain and are uncomfortable doing so. Yet in many cultures, the locals think we're crazy if we don't bargain. My wife is a terrific bargainer. All Filipinos are. I, on the other hand, am true to my German heritage and a lousy bargainer.

Case in point. While on a business trip to Seoul, South Korea,

I went shopping on my last day to find a dress for Fe. I entered a tiny shop and spotted just what I wanted: a lovely black and white, silk dress hanging from on overhead rack. I tried not to look too excited when I asked the shopkeeper the price. The woman spoke no English, but I could tell from the way her eyes stirred that she sensed my interest. She quickly wrote a figure down on a piece of paper: $125. I knew that was just an opening figure and that I was expected to bargain, so I studied her timeworn face for a moment before countering with an offer of $75. Before long, we had settled on a price of $90, and I felt good about my bargaining prowess. I was certain Fe would be proud of me.

There was only one problem. The shop owner didn't accept credit cards, and I only had $30 left in Korean won. Fortunately, the shop owner's daughter arrived at that moment. She spoke sufficient English to explain this to her mother who immediately dropped the price to $80, thinking that I was still negotiating. This surprised and pleased me, but it still left me $50 short. I told her that I would return to my hotel to see if I could get cash from my credit card. This was before debit cards were invented, but I had charged cash to my credit card in places like Ushuaia, Argentina, and I figured if a place at the tip of South America was willing to advance me money on my credit card, surely the Koreans would do the same.

The shop owner was not about to let me out of her sight, however, and told her daughter to accompany me with the dress. Off we went to my hotel, where I soon discovered that I couldn't make the exchange. Disappointed, I told the daughter that I couldn't buy the dress. She phoned her mother at once with the news, and guess what? Rather than return the dress to the shop -- maybe it was considered bad luck -- she gave it to me for the $30! And there in a nut shell is the difference in cultures when it comes to bargaining. I'd stopped at $90; Fe would have driven the final price much lower.

Sometimes, superstitions are wrapped up in the country's culture. In Punta Arenas, a small town found not too far from Ushuaia at the southern tip of Chile, there is a park with a bronze statue of a man whose naked foot dangles within reach of passersby. Local people walking through the park stop to rub or kiss the statue's toe. Mothers even lift up their children so they can reach the toe. The locals believe that by doing this, they will return in a future life, and the toe shines as brilliantly as polished brass from all the rubbing and kissing. The concept is eerily similar to one of the basic premises of Buddhism -- preparing for one's future life.

The toe in Punta Arenas reminded me of a bronze sculpture I had seen on St. Charles Bridge in Prague. It depicted the story of St. John Nepomik who was thrown to his death from the bridge in 1393. He was canonized in 1729 and since then Catholics have been reverently touching the figure of the saint who is portrayed in the act of being cast from the bridge. Like the toe, the image of St. John Nepomik gleams as if by divine light, only this time the gesture is one of devotion, not superstition.

Remember those hanging graves in Torajaland, Indonesia? There's more to their story, and it speaks directly to our conversations about culture. Torajans don't bury their dead until the proper funeral rites can be held for neighbors and relatives. When the family is poor, it may be a year or longer before a formal burial can take place. That's because the family must first raise the money to sacrifice a water buffalo and to hold a small feast. In the meantime, the deceased lies in the house in a state of semi-mummification.

For a wealthy family, the event is much more elaborate, and it happens a lot sooner. First, a small village of houses shaped like long boats on stilts is built. Next, pigs are slaughtered and cooked over open fires while the arriving guests sit around drinking rice wine, smoking cigarettes, and chatting with neighbors and friends. Actually, the pigs aren't so much cooked as singed. They are tossed on the fires, turned over a couple of times, then cut into bloody pieces that are eaten almost raw. Pretty soon the grassy area in front of the long houses is soaked with blood, but no one seems to mind. The rice wine has been flowing freely, and expressions have become glassy-eyed. The number of pigs offered by the family is a sign of their status and wealth, so the more the better. The number often exceeds forty. The festival lasts about three days, during which time everybody climbs the steps of the main house to pay their respects to the departed.

Including me! At the family's behest, I climbed the stairs and entered a warm room cast in deep shadows. The air carried a stale odor that I associated with Egyptian tombs. I was surprised to find a woman seated by the mummified body, which lay on a dais wrapped in cloth, but apparently this was common practice. Someone always remained by the body's side until the spirit was released from its worldly realm. She nodded her head to me and murmured a greeting. As I studied the remains of the deceased, I marveled at the parallels found in cultures around the world. Here I was in the highlands of Sulawesi, Indonesia, visiting a culture that could only be reached by driving for hours over nearly non-existent roads, and observing a mummified body much like the ones found in Egyptian museums.

When the funeral festival is over, the village of long houses is abandoned. Wander through Torajaland, and you'll discover many crumbling villages that are slowly being reclaimed by the area's lush foliage.

Here's the strange thing about the ceremony I've just described. The exact same kind of festival is held for weddings, without the corpse, of course. I was lucky enough to attend a wedding festival the next day, and I saw scenes so similar, it was difficult to tell the difference.

It's interesting to consider how the Torajan's culture regarding burials compares with India's customs regarding cremations. When someone dies in India, the body must be cremated within twenty-four hours. Quite a contrast to the Torajans, where a body might remain unburied for a year or more! Of course, India has its own rituals. One of them involves collecting the ashes and bones from the funeral pyre and immersing them in the holy waters of the Ganges River. Ground zero for this ceremony is on the banks of the sacred river in Varanasi. An estimated twenty thousand pilgrims arrive there each day to perform the required purifying rituals before scattering the ashes of their loved ones on the holy water.

For those who are lucky enough to live less than a day away from the Ganges, bodies are wrapped and brought directly to the holy river, where they are immersed in the water before cremation. The cremation ghats are busy twenty-four hours a day, but they are particularly breathtaking at night when dozens of fires can be seen burning on the steps beside the river. This is also the time to witness the colorful "aarti" ceremony, a vibrant, spiritual feast for the eyes and ears that takes place each evening immediately adjacent to the funeral pyres. Five young priests stand on platforms along the banks of the Ganges, where they offer fire to Lord Shiva and perform ritual tasks with incense and camphor, accompanied by a cacophony of ringing bells and musical voices. One man twirled a hammer in one hand then banged it against a bell he held in the other. He repeated this small ceremony again and again, never losing his beat or the smile of ecstasy on his face. Standing there watching the priests' hypnotic movements and listening to the mesmerizing sounds of the bells and voices, I felt a spiritual energy washing over me as powerful as ocean waves pounding the shore.

The scenes I've just described bring religion into the cultural equation and blur the lines of culture even further. Where does one begin and the other end? That's open to individual interpretation, I suppose, and I won't attempt to answer the question here. Before things get any more confusing, let me end this chapter with an incident that has culture written all over it. For that, we will return to Tibet.

My mini-group had just climbed through the Himalayas in our little van, and we were about to enter the Tibetan plateau when we came upon a small glacier that stretched across the road. Enterprising Tibetans had chopped a passageway through the wall of living ice just large enough for one vehicle to pass through at a time. Unfortunately, all the vans and lorries were stopped, and no one was moving. It didn't take long to discover the reason for the delay. A lorry with a full load of wooden crates had buried its right-front wheel in a pothole smack in the middle of the passageway. It leaned drunkenly to one side, its cargo resting precariously against the glacier's wall. Traffic was blocked in both directions, and several Tibetan drivers were squatted beside the stricken truck smoking cigarettes and chatting. One man casually tossed rocks into the pothole around the trapped wheel. A raw wind whipped through the chasm, but it didn't seem to affect the Tibetans. They could have just as easily been sunning themselves on the beach as sitting on their heels in this godforsaken place. They didn't appear to have a care in the world.

My guide informed us that we would have to wait until a lorry appeared with a heavy enough load to pull the truck from its prison. How long would that be, I asked? The guide raised his shoulders in the manner of someone who hadn't a clue. More lorries arrived, but none had the weight necessary to rescue the hapless truck. Engines coughed to a halt, and more drivers gathered on both sides of the glacier, where they laughed and shared smokes while the minutes flew by. It was fascinating to see how completely unfazed they were by the delay. Time had little relevance in their world. They had no watches or deadlines. Whether they waited an hour or a day didn't matter. That was my first lesson in Tibetan culture. Time, as I knew it, had no relevance to theirs.

We waited an hour for the proper lorry to arrive, and that was when I got my second lesson in Tibetan culture. A long line had formed on either side of the glacier, and heads rose expectantly when a new driver with a heavy load stopped his lorry at the back of the line and shut off his engine. At last, our rescuer was at hand! Several drivers approached the man and asked him to help, but the driver refused. He remained seated in his cab, content to wait for another lorry! I found his response frustrating, but I was equally intrigued by the reaction of the other drivers. Instead of losing patience and shouting at him, they laughed and cajoled the obstinate man, all the while urging him to come forward. At first, the man wouldn't budge, but the drivers' strategy eventually worked. The man finally relented and drove his heavy truck to the front of the line. A chain large enough to hold a ship's anchor was quickly produced, and several men happily attached it to the axles of the stricken lorry and the one that had just arrived. Amid shouts and much fanfare, the crippled lorry was pulled from the hole with its load still intact. After more than an hour of delays, it had taken less than five minutes to clear the road through the glacier, and the Tibetans had never shown any anger or frustration about their dilemma.

There were, I decided, a lot of things we could learn from those cavalier men.

## CHAPTER TEN
## *THE HIGHWAY CODE OF INDIA*

This chapter is about surviving the traffic and driving conditions in the countries we visit. Survival is definitely the operative word in India. Shortly after we arrived, our guide, Shailesh, shared his Highway Code of India with us. The code was developed by Shailesh and some friends to provide humorous insights into how people drive in his country, and Fe and I found it terribly amusing . . . until we ventured out and actually immersed ourselves in the sea of honking horns, sacred cows, two-stroke tuk tuks, taxis, cars, trucks, buses, rickshaws, and camel-drawn carts that seemed to occupy every square inch of the roadways. It was then that we began to appreciate Shailesh's code, and it seemed like the perfect introduction to this chapter. So here it is.

THE HIGHWAY CODE OF INDIA
Article I: The assumption of immortality is required of all road users.

Article II:  Indian traffic, like Indian society, is structured on a strict caste system.  In descending order, give way to cows, elephants, camels, buffalos, pigs/goats/dogs, heavy trucks, buses, official cars, pedal rickshaws, private cars, motorcycles, scooters, auto-rickshaws, handcarts, and pedestrians.

Article III: All wheeled vehicles shall be driven in accordance with the following manifesto: to slow is to falter; to brake is to fail; to stop is to be defeated.

Article IV: Use of the horn.

Cars: short blasts (urgent) indicate supremacy for clearing dogs, rickshaws and pedestrians from one's path.  Long blasts (desperate) indicate impending disaster.  (I am going too fast to stop, so unless you slow down we shall both die.) In extreme cases, this may be accompanied by flashing headlights. A single blast (casual) may mean "I have seen somebody I know" or "I haven't blown my horn for several minutes."

Trucks and buses: all horn signals have the same meaning. "I weigh up to 12.5 tons and have no intention of stopping even if I could." This signal may be emphasized by the use of headlights.

Article V: All maneuvers, use of horn, and evasive actions shall be left until the last possible moment.

Article VI: Traffic entering a road from the left has right of way. So has traffic entering from the right, and also traffic in the middle.

Article VII: Traffic islands in the middle of crossroads have no traffic function and should be ignored.

Article VIII: Overtaking is mandatory. Every moving vehicle is required to overtake. This should be done under suitable conditions, such as in the face of oncoming traffic, on blind curves, and in the middle of villages/city centers. No more than two inches should be allowed between your vehicle and the one you are passing.  In the case of bicycles or pedestrians, allow one inch.

Article IX: Nirvana may be obtained through the head-on crash.

Article X: Putting your car in reverse is almost unheard of and against the driver's mantra.

Everywhere we drove in India, the above articles proved themselves again and again, and it didn't help to see the occasional wrecked car or truck crumpled by the side of the road. Miraculously, we survived the two inch rule and all of the others and arrived back in Delhi at the end of our journey unscathed. I was indebted to Shailesh for sharing his highway code and for all those truck drivers who swerved back into their lanes at the last possible moment.

Now that we have been introduced to India's driving idiosyncrasies, let's look at some others.

### CAIRO, EGYPT

I probably need to put a great big asterisk on this one because of the change in government, but I suspect that for the short term at least, little has changed. Cairo is a city with so many personalities, it leaves you not only breathing in another language but uttering a few choice words as well. You can thank Cairo's traffic for the latter. It can turn your world upside down. No one pays any attention to the traffic laws, and everyone drives with their horns instead of their brakes. The result is a constant cacophony of honking cars, day and night. And just try crossing a street on foot. Pedestrians in Cairo have a lot in common with those who run with the bulls in Pamplona, Spain. One moment an opening appears and you think it's safe; the next, you are running for your life as vehicles of every size, shape and color swoop down on you, all honking their horns. How about street lights, you ask? Just try to find one, and when you do, don't bother with it. Red or green has little meaning to these rumbling gladiators. What about traffic cops? It's true, there used to be an average of at least one policeman per corner before Mubarak was tossed, but most of them were snoozing in the shade of their tiny guard stations or talking to each other. O.K. you say, if you can't lick them, why not rent a car and join them? Bad idea. Driving in Cairo is the equivalent of diving into a thundering river when you don't know how to swim. Your odds are better running with the bulls.

Traffic aside, Cairo has some other interesting idiosyncrasies.

One is the sheer number of people who reside there, which is one reason for the horrendous traffic. To accommodate the rapidly expanding population, city officials have allowed builders to throw up concrete slabs of apartment buildings all the way to the pyramids, which make visiting those timeless wonders a bit disconcerting. When you stand near the pyramids and look to the left, all you will see is an endless desert stretching to the horizon. Look to your right, and all you will see is an endless sea of roof tops. Most of those rooftops are unfinished, I might add. That's due to a quirk in the tax laws that says unfinished buildings are not charged property taxes. So families build multi-story dwellings and leave steel rods sticking out the top of them to show they plan to add more floors. They don't, of course, but as long as they declare their intent, they're not assessed property taxes. I'm told the tax laws are changing to close this loophole.

Then there is the City of the Dead, an immense cemetery right in the middle of Cairo. There's enough room there to transplant all the pyramids in Egypt, but the size of the place isn't the only point of interest. Over population has driven many of the poorest residents to move there. There are now so many people residing in the cemetery that the government has built mosques for prayers and a school for children. The City of the Dead has become the city of the living!

### SEOUL, SOUTH KOREA

Of course, India doesn't have an exclusive on highway codes. The Article for the following might read: Beware of taxi drivers who take back streets . . .

My taxi driver was mumbling to himself, and I could see why. I had just arrived in Seoul, and I was sitting in a cab on my way into the city from the airport. Except we weren't moving. Traffic was terrible, much worse than I recalled when I first visited the country two weeks earlier. Then, it had taken less than thirty minutes to reach the Seoul Plaza Hotel in the downtown area. It was apparent that it would take quite a bit longer this time. What could be the matter, I wondered? There was no point in asking my driver; he didn't speak a word of English. It crossed my mind that he might be taking me by some back route to run up the tab, but I saw enough familiar landmarks to tell me that we were headed in the right direction. There were just a lot more cars on the road this time, much like Los Angeles at rush hour.

In desperation, my driver left the main road, and started winding through secondary streets. Now I *was* lost and had little choice but to put my trust in this chain-smoking man who attacked the traffic as if his personal honor was at stake. He would thrust one way and parry another, squeeze down an alleyway, or zig-zag through a maze of tiny streets where people stared with curiosity as we wiggled past them. I sensed that we were making progress, although I had nothing on which to base my intuition other than the fact that my driver had stopped mumbling.

Then, something magical happened. He had just scooted down a street so narrow there was barely room for the taxi to squeeze past rows of vendors selling hogs heads, fresh fish, and other delicacies along the sidewalks, when we suddenly popped out of a side street and onto the broad boulevard that ran from the Namdaemun Gate straight to my hotel. The boulevard was at least ten lanes wide, and we were the only car on it. Both sides of the road were lined with throngs of people who waved and called to us as we passed. Soldiers with grave expressions guarded every street corner to prevent wayward cars like ours from entering the street, and more than a few of them registered their shock as we whizzed past. Clearly, we didn't belong there, and I half-expected the soldiers to either wave us down or to start shooting at us. Thankfully, neither happened, and my driver sped up the middle of the empty boulevard as fast as he could. As soon as we arrived at the Seoul Plaza Hotel, I paid the driver, and he disappeared around the corner into the back streets before anyone could question him. It didn't take long to learn why my driver was so worried. The South Korean President, Chun Doo Wan, and his entourage were scheduled to drive up the same street in a matter of minutes. Somehow, my taxi driver had found the only unguarded entrance to the boulevard, and we had just upstaged the country's president!

I didn't want anybody asking me questions either, so I checked in as quickly as possible and fled to my room.

COSTA RICA

In Costa Rica, I should have followed Article X from India: Never back up. Fe and I had decided to rent a car and drive around Costa Rica for a couple of weeks. It seemed like a good idea until we hit the road, literally. It turned out that Costa Rica had some of the worst roads in the world. All the cars had four wheel drive, and even that didn't help much at times. Why the rough ride? Not only were most of the roads unpaved, they were so primitive it felt like the Jolly Green Giant had taken a jackhammer to the place. In fact, the roads were so bad insurance companies refused to offer auto coverage. Instead, we were required to put an $800 deposit on our credit card to cover potential damages. As long as there was no damage to the car, we wouldn't be charged anything extra. Otherwise, we could most likely say goodbye to our $800. My hands twitched a bit as I handed over my credit card, but what the heck, it had been years since I'd had any rental car problems. What could possibly go wrong . . . go wrong . . . go wrong?

Off we drove, and at first things went smoothly. Well, not smoothly, exactly. The paved roads out of the country's capital, San Jose, quickly vanished, to be replaced by teeth-rattling beds of volcanic rock that seemed determined to tear our little car to pieces. The car held together, however, and we rolled through the countryside without incident . . . until I saw some fieldworkers and decided to photograph them. I slammed on the brakes, put the car in reverse, and backed up, unaware of a stone bridge hidden from my view by foliage. I plowed into the hidden bridge with the force of a bull elephant during mating season.

When I jumped out to inspect the carnage, I instantly thought about the $800 on my credit card and imagined it flying away on tiny wings. The rear axle was bent at an angle that reminded me of a badly broken leg, and the back bumper was jammed so tightly against the tire, it wouldn't turn. The car wasn't going anywhere, and I feared it might be a day or two before help arrived. Most of

Costa Rica consisted of back roads such as the one we were on. There were few villages. More to the point, I hadn't seen any sign of a towing service since we left San Jose. The Auto Club wasn't going to come to our rescue.

As I stood there mulling over my options (or lack thereof), an elderly man who had watched my saga wandered over to have a look. He tsk tsked at me, mumbled something I couldn't comprehend, and wandered away. I figured I had given him a good laugh and would never see him again, but he returned a short time later with a crow bar. After considerable exertion, I managed to pry the bumper just far enough away from the tire to allow the wheel to rotate. After I thanked and tipped the old man, we hopped into the car and limped away.

We weren't going to get very far, however. The bumper still rubbed against the tire, creating a shrill chafing noise that assaulted our eardrums and so much white smoke from the tire, it looked like we were sending smoke signals home to the States. Things didn't look promising; it wouldn't take long for that bumper to tear the tire to shreds.

The nice thing about foreign travel is that little miracles do happen from time-to-time. Our miracle appeared in the form of a small town that sprang out of nowhere. The town didn't look like much, but as we approached in our cloud of smoke, we saw what looked like a service station. There was a rusted gas pump leaning in Tower of Pisa fashion by the side of the road, and a garage with a large truck parked inside. The truck was rusting as badly as the gas pump and looked like it hadn't been moved in months, if not years. It was a stretch to call the place a service station, but I was desperate.

When we stopped, a wiry man in overalls promptly emerged from the garage wiping his hands on an oily cloth. He introduced himself as the owner/mechanic of the fine establishment and quickly inspected the damage. When he was done, he mumbled something just as incomprehensible as the old man on the road and waved me over to the truck, from which he produced a long chain with a large hook on either end. Sound familiar? Images of Tibet and that lorry caught in the glacier instantly sprang to mind. The owner/mechanic attached one end to the axel of the truck and the other end to my bent axel. Next, he positioned my car so there was about ten feet of slack in the chain. Finally, he told me in broken English to start the engine of my car and accelerate as fast as I could from a standing start. My mind quickly reeled through the possible outcomes of such a violent action while my inner voices screamed at me not to do it. However, the man seemed pretty sure of himself, and what the hell, I had nothing to lose. The car wasn't going anywhere in its current condition, and I wasn't going to see that $800 deposit again anyway. How much more damage could I do?

So, I floored the accelerator, popped the clutch and charged ahead. Bam! My teeth rattled and my head bounced off the head rest as the car leaped at least a foot off the ground and stopped. The mechanic inspected the axle and signaled for me to go again. Bam! Now my ears were ringing, and I was beginning to question my sanity. The mechanic gave me a thumbs up and signaled for me to go one more time. Bam! Little birds started flying around my head.

The mechanic grinned as he continued to wipe his hands on his oily rag and told me the problem was fixed. I didn't dare look under the car. I smiled weakly, instead, and asked how much I owed him for the repair. He shook his head. No charge, he said. He was glad he could help. I suspected he'd had so much fun watching me beat my brains out that he didn't have the heart to take my money. It was a nice gesture, however, and I thanked him.

Off we went again. The billowing white smoke had disappeared, and the shrill chafing sound had been replaced by a thin whining noise that sounded like we were being pursued by an angry bee. I never backed up again the rest of our trip, which thankfully proceeded as planned. By the time we had returned to San Jose, the rear tire was torn assunder. I knew we'd experienced a little more excitement than planned, but thanks to that auto mechanic our trip had been saved.

You can imagine my trepidation when we returned home,

however. That $800 credit card charge loomed over my head each day as I opened my mail box and looked for my credit card statement. When it finally arrived, I left it unopened on the dining room table for more than an hour before I mustered the courage to look at it. The charge was extraordinary, but not in the way I expected. The total due for all the damage I had done to the rear end of that car was only $187. I could have spent that much changing a tire in Germany. Costa Rica was an amazingly inexpensive country, and I can definitely recommend driving there, even if the roads are nearly impassable in places. But take my advice and don't back up!

SCOTLAND

The first time I tried renting and driving a car in another country was many years ago in Scotland, and I must confess that I suffered from a severe case of overconfidence. After all, everybody spoke English, although that didn't necessarily mean that I could understand what they said, and the signs were easy to read, except for a few with some rather strange phrases that I had to translate, like "roundabout" and "lay about." And, of course, all the cars had their steering wheels on the wrong side of the car, and everybody drove on the wrong side of the road (left side instead of right). That meant that I had to sit on the right side of the car and shift gears with my left hand while I also drove on the wrong side of the road. I found these quirks a bit disconcerting, but they in no way undermined my sense of adventure.

The car I rented happened to be a small, blue one that reminded me of my blue sports car back home. My first mistake was to confuse the two. In no time at all, I was whizzing along with no idea how close I was coming to sideswiping the parked cars on my left. I was employing the "two inch rule" and didn't even know it! My next mistake was not understanding that vehicles in a "roundabout" had the right away. For those who have not experienced one of these circular whirling dervishes, roundabouts are used instead of signals to control the flow of traffic at intersections. The idea is to enter the circle, then drive in circles until you can figure out where to exit.

I entered my first roundabout in front of a very large bus, whose blaring horn informed me that I had just ignored its right-of-way and I was about to be squashed like a bug. Fortunately, the bus' brakes worked as well as its horn, and I escaped with little more than an anxiety attack and damaged pride. Imagine how I felt. How would you like to have a bus blasting its horn at you the first day you are driving on the wrong side of the road, sitting in the wrong side of the car, and shifting with the wrong hand? I won't even talk about later that day when I looked the wrong way and almost pulled in front of an even larger truck.

The real point of this story is what happened the following day. I had stayed at a bed and breakfast on the edge of town, and I rose the next morning to the delicious smells of a sumptuous breakfast, where I enjoyed fresh ham and bread and learned to knock the tops off soft-boiled eggs sitting in egg cups. After breakfast, I packed my bags, and bid my hosts farewell. Off I roared in my little blue car . . . for two blocks. At that point, the two inch rule abandoned me, and I ran over the razor-sharp edge of a stone curb, blowing out both the left front and rear tires. Once again, I had misjudged distances on my left because I was seated on the right. Red-faced, humbled, and embarrassed, I trudged back to the B&B I had just vacated and phoned the car rental agency. Good news! The airport office was close by, and since I'd been wise enough to pay for full-collision coverage, a driver delivered a replacement car to my B&B within a quarter hour at no additional charge. The new car was not blue and did not remind me of my sports car, which was just as well. I had been thoroughly chastened by my mistakes and had no desire of repeating them.

BHUTAN

I didn't have to drive when I visited Bhutan, which was a good thing, but there were still lots of idiosyncrasies and driving adventures. To begin, the entire country of Bhutan had only one main road. It consisted of a single lane that was patched and blacktopped from one end of the country to the other. The road ran all the way from the western town of Paro, site of the country's only airport, to Tashigang, the country's last town of any size before you banged into the top of India. I was there on a photographic assignment, and the only way to cover the breadth of the country was to drive across it and back again. That posed interesting challenges, some physical and some psychological.

First, the psychological. I had a driver and guide, both of whom were competent and pleasant, but they only had one music tape, which they played incessantly during the seven day journey. Not only did I come to know every note in every song by heart, I could honestly say that by the seventh day, my sanity was on the verge of deserting me. Chinese water torture would have been less painful.

Next, the physical challenges. Here I'm referring to that single ribbon of blacktop that we used to traverse the country. Every winter, the road was bombarded by boulders and washed out by heavy rains and snow at hundreds of locations. Laborers arrived from India and Nepal each spring to fix the damage. They spent the entire spring and summer repairing the road, and usually finished just in time for the next winter season. It was an endless cycle of destruction and repair, and it made driving an endless cycle of hurry-up-and-wait. We would drive for several miles at moderate speeds, then slow to a crawl as we picked our way around boulders and past workmen who appeared to be covered in more layers of slick tar than the road.

It was the final challenge, however, that offered the most thrills. Like India, Bhutan was one of those countries that tested the laws of physics, specifically the one that states "no two objects can occupy the same space at the same time." As I said before, the road was only one lane wide, and we had to ascend and descend dozens of mountain passes filled with blind curves. In order to stay alive, the driver had to constantly honk his horn to alert any oncoming traffic that we were there. If we didn't hear a reply, we assumed it was safe to proceed. When we did hear another horn, we crept forward cautiously and tried to pass the other vehicle without tumbling over the sheer cliffs that frequented our route.

Most of the traffic that we met consisted of very large trucks, and while they were not as wild as the ones we faced in India, they still commanded the center of the road. We couldn't defy the physics of two objects occupying one space, so we followed the two inch rule instead. Whenever we met a truck, our little car was squeezed to within two inches of the cliff!

It turned out that the King of Bhutan was just as concerned as I was about the country's traffic conditions, and he had signs posted along the road urging drivers to use caution. One of my favorites was: No Hurry No Worry. English was the second language of Bhutan, by the way, so the signs were all in English.

### KATHMANDU, NEPAL

In many countries, honking the horn is as natural as bowing to one another or shaking hands. India's maniacal truck drivers even had signs painted on the backs of their trucks *asking* you to blow your horn so they would know you were there. People honked all the time, but not in anger. It was simply how they communicated, and let's face it, if you were going to employ the two inch rule, you had to communicate.

In Nepal's capital, Kathmandu, it was nearly impossible to move without a horn. I learned this when my driver entered the Thamel District, a warren of narrow streets mobbed with pedestrians, rickshaws, cars, and trucks, all of which shimmied their way in bumps and grinds with total disregard for the traffic around them. The only way to clear a path through this chaos was to constantly blow one's horn, but our car's horn had suddenly stopped working. There we sat in a sea of humanity, and we could hardly budge. Without our horn, we became invisible. It made me think of an additional proclamation for Article IV of Shailesh's Highway Code of India: Never underestimate the power of the horn.

### POTPURRI

There have been so many driving mishaps and experiences over the years, it's hard to cover them all, so I won't. But I thought it might be amusing to compare a few of the driving idiosyncrasies found around the world. Let's start in Manila, Philippines. There was too much traffic for cars to go terribly fast in Manila, but drivers made up for this by the way they drove. Cars flowed back and forth across lanes of traffic as if no one else was there. A driver would change lanes without looking, steering his car right into the one alongside him. In an instant, both the two inch rule and the law of physics about two occupying objects were tossed in the compost bin. Those two cars *had* to occupy the same space at the same time. There was no other way to explain it, until I realized that the invaded car had somehow shifted lanes before a collision took place and was now invading the space of another driver who also shied away, only this time into the oncoming traffic. A head-on collision seemed inevitable, but nothing of the sort happened. The cars on the other side of the road shifted out of harms way, as well. In this manner, cars floated away from each other in a dance of continuous chain reactions that salvaged both of the above-mentioned rules from the compost bin and put the world back in order. The traffic patterns reminded me of fields of wheat flowing in the wind. First, the wind blew the stalks one way, then it blew them another.

I had always heard what daring drivers the Italians were, and I must admit to some trepidation when I first drove there. What I quickly discovered, however, was that if I stayed away from the larger cities, the Italian drivers weren't that bad, except for their habit of leaping out at me from side roads, then stopping at the last moment as I drove past. That nearly gave me heart failure until I got used to it. The cities were much more challenging, although even there I found the chaos to be manageable. I must, however, add one very large asterisk to my assessment of driving in Italy. *It does not include Rome. Never drive in Rome unless you are: 1) schizophrenic, 2) young and don't give a damn, or 3) harboring a secret death wish.

Gladiators in the Roman Forum stood a better chance of survival than foreign drivers on the streets of Rome, where cars often lined up five and six across at a red light, then waged a fierce battle that could be categorized somewhere between drag racing and demolition derby as everyone tried to be the first to reach one of the three lanes on the other side of the intersection. It was even more dangerous for pedestrians. I once saw a dozen nuns preparing to cross the street that circles the Coliseum and decided it would be safer to join them than to attempt the crossing on my own. If traffic was going to stop for anyone, it would be a group of nuns, right? We waited until a gap appeared in the stampede of cars, trucks, and motorbikes, then stepped into the street and hurried on our way. We were less than half-way across when another wave of metallic beasts bore down on us. The nuns picked up their pace, and so did I. Not only were the cars not stopping for us, they weren't even slowing down! With robes flying and feet pounding, the nuns sprinted the last few yards to safety with me right on their heels. We all stopped on the sidewalk and inhaled deeply, partly to catch our breaths and partly to acknowledge our small victory. Visions of the movie Mad Max starring Mel Gibson came to mind; I couldn't help wondering if Rome had inspired the movie's road racing scenes.

If you want the perfect contrast to the Italian driver, go to Germany. There, everything is very orderly but very *fast*. Germans live with precision, and they drive that way. Take the Autobahn where speeds can exceed one hundred and twenty miles per hour. Speed restrictions do exist, but that hardly seems to affect the mentality of the German driver. There are rules and protocols, however. In the U.S., for example, we think nothing of hopping into the left hand lane on a highway and staying there even when cars approach behind us. Do that on the Autobahn in Germany, and you will have headlights flashing in your rearview mirror before you can say "was ist das?." The left lane is only for passing slower cars or for driving at the speed of light. So, if you want to keep your sanity, stay to the right.

I almost lost *my* sanity one time, and I wasn't on the Autobahn. In the first chapter I mentioned Fe's sister, Vicky, who lives near Munich. We try to visit her and her family every two or three years. On one trip, we were met at the Munich airport by

Vicky and a neighbor's son who had offered to pick us up. The drive through Munich was uneventful, but once we hit the country roads, the young man put on the afterburners and streaked along the two-lane road at speeds approaching a hundred miles an hour! I had the pleasure of sitting next to him in the front seat, and all I could think about, as the lush, Bavarian scenery whizzed past my window in a blur, was that a car, tractor, or cow was bound to appear in our lane at any moment. The young man was a very good driver, but that didn't stop me from recalling that law of physics about no two objects. When the speedometer exceeded one hundred and fifty kilometers per hour, I decided it was best to simply close my eyes.

Oh, and one more thing. It's illegal to pass on the right.

# CHAPTER ELEVEN
## *I PRAY, THEREFORE I AM*

The woman wore a simple, gray skirt and sweater, and a cloth bag hung from her neck to waist level. She was barefoot and of an indiscernible age, anywhere from thirty to fifty. I had just entered the courtyard of the Pelkor Chode monastery in Gyantse, Tibet, and the woman was the first person I noticed. She stood, head bowed, in front of the main entrance to the monastery with her hands pressed before her in prayer. As I watched, she raised her hands above her head, then lowered them as she fell to her knees and sprawled on her stomach on the entryway's cold, unyielding stones. As she stretched out on the ground, she slipped her hands into leather straps lying before her so that she wouldn't scrape her palms raw on the stones, and she did it all in one, graceful motion. Moments passed. The air was chilled with frost. The stones on which she lay must have felt like sheets of ice piercing her rough clothing. Slowly, the woman rose to her feet and began the ritual again.

I had arrived in the town of Gyantse to see the remains of its famous Gyantse Dzong, a fortress which had stood for centuries before being destroyed by Mao Tse Tung's Red Guard during China's cultural revolution. Broken walls and building remnants were all that remained.

Miraculously, Gyantse's Pelkor Chode monastery and Kumbum Stupa had survived the Red Guard's onslaught. The stupa was of particular interest to me. Stupas were built to house important religious objects, such as manuscripts and statues of Buddha, or the remains of a revered lama, including hair clippings and cremated ashes. I had visited two stupas near Kathmandu in Nepal and would discover several more in Bhutan, but this was the only major one I would see in Tibet. Most stupas looked like rounded pyramids, but the Kumbum Stupa had a ribbed design formed by outside walkways that ringed each of its five floors in zigzag patterns. They reminded me of the angular walkways used by the Chinese to keep evil spirits from reaching their famous teahouse in Shanghai. Tibet was such a spiritual country, I couldn't help wondering if the stupa's ribbed design had a similar purpose.

Near the peak of the stupa, a pair of narrowed eyes stared down on me. The eyes were painted on each of the four sides of the stupa, and I could feel them following me as I walked around the structure's base. The eyes symbolized the eyes of Buddha and were considered beneficent to the pilgrims and villagers who prayed there, but I had the unsettling feeling that they were watching me with suspicion. They pierced my skin much like I imagined the cold stones piercing the skin of that woman praying in front of the monastery.

Steep, wooden ladders allowed me access to the various floors of the stupa, where a series of tiny, outside chapels housed religious images, including Buddha, Guru Rinpoche, and various disciples. Guru Rinpoche was a monumental figure in Tibetan and Bhutanese folklore. He was credited with founding Tibet's first monastery, the Samye, and with flying into Bhutan on the back of a tiger to establish the Taksang Monastery, also known as the Tiger's Nest. Blessed with mythical powers, he was considered by many to be the second Buddha.

After exploring the Kumbum Stupa, I entered the monastery, where I found four monks praying along one wall. A thin, grey light fought its way into the room through the doorway near where they sat. The light wrestled with the bruised, blue-black shadows that filled much of the room, but the shadows had the upper hand. The subdued glow of several butter lamps softened the shadows and provided enough light to highlight the statue of Buddha which sat serenely above the main altar. I desperately wanted to photograph the monks, but that would have meant using a flash, and I felt certain the monks would not allow it. So, I contented myself with listening to the rhythm of their drum beats and voices and marveling at the magical atmosphere created by the many spirits I felt certain were flying around the room.

When I left the monastery, the wind had increased noticeably, and the air had become even more chilled than before. I immediately looked for the praying woman, and there she was, right where I had seen her when I first entered the courtyard. She was still genuflecting and sprawling across those icy stones. More than an hour had passed since my arrival. How long she had been there before I came, I didn't know, but if I understood her body language, she would be there long after I was gone.

Some of the most compelling images we are likely to see when we travel are the rituals and devotions expressed by people according to their religious beliefs. There is a spirit in every culture that cries out for understanding, a spirit that seems best understood by expressing one's fealty to a god or afterlife, whether that entails reaching heaven or attaining nirvana.

Churches, temples, monasteries, and mosques make up an important part of this experience. In Bavarian, Germany, church ceilings and walls are often set ablaze with brilliantly colored frescoes set against snowy white backgrounds; elaborate alters are adorned with saints and spiraling angels; and elegant organs float on balconies above the main entrances. The Sistine Chapel in the Vatican has inspired laymen and priests for centuries with stories of the bible as visualized by Michelangelo. Inside Moscow's

Kremlin, the Square of Cathedrals presents a gathering of churches unlike any other in the world. Gleaming, golden domes and Ivan the Great's bell tower reach heavenward. Gilded archways provide graceful backdrops to breathless displays of murals and wood-paneled chapels, which are found in abundance inside each of the five main cathedrals: Archangel, Annunciation, Assumption, Upper Savior, and Twelve Apostles. Ivan the Great's son, Ivan the Terrible, prayed there for forgiveness from his infamous sins, and when the priests banned him from praying at the alter of the Cathedral of the Annunciation, he had a separate alter built onto the side of the church for his personal use.

Standing just outside the Kremlin's walls in Red Square is one of the most celebrated churches in the world, the Cathedral of St. Basil the Blessed, whose eight, vivid onion domes rise into the sky like primeval roman candles. St. Basil was designed and built to commemorate Russia's conquest of the tartars, and each of the eight domes symbolized one of Ivan the Terrible's victories. Ivan found the cathedral so exquisite, he had the architects blinded so they could never build a church to rival St. Basil's beauty.

If there *is* a church to rival St. Basil, it might be the Basilica of St. Marks, a fairytale structure found in Venice's Piazza San Marcos square. The church was built over several centuries as Venice's wealth and trade dominance grew, and the result is an amazing variety of décor that includes gold, mosaic-lined walls and precious marble columns inside, and an exterior roof that boasts more oriental domes, spires, and statues than stars in the heavens.

During one of my visits to Venice, a first communion was held for children in the square in front of St. Marks. The children were dressed in a sea of white, offering a stark contrast to the black habits of the nuns seated near the arched entryway of St. Marks. An elaborate brass altar displaying reliefs of the apostles and covered in white linen stood between two towering candle holders on the top step. Hundreds of proud parents and spectators sat in folding chairs arranged in long, neat rows, while throngs of bystanders crowded around the perimeter or wandered through the square behind us. The children giggled and whispered to one another while the priests performed their ceremonies behind the brass altar. I sauntered happily through the maze of habits and faces photographing many special images, until one of the ushers realized that I was not a sanctioned photographer and politely asked me to take my seat.

On another occasion, I attended a mass inside St. Marks. The ceremony was bathed in the golden light of candles reflecting off the mosaic walls. The standing-room-only crowd of worshippers listened in rapture to the priest's singsong prayers as they slowly drifted up into the lofty domed ceiling overhead. I had never witnessed anything so compelling before in my life . . . until I attended those ceremonies along the Ganges River that I described in Chapter Eight.

As much as I enjoy visiting churches and other religious sanctuaries around the world, I find the religious ceremonies themselves even more fascinating and moving. At the Church of the Miracle of Guadalupe in Mexico City, for example, I have watched worshippers crawl on their knees across more than a hundred yards of unforgiving concrete to the church's main entrance. Similarly, people crawled on their knees down the aisle from the entrance of the Church of Los Angeles in Costa Rica. Everyone, from the elderly to young fathers and mothers carrying babies in their arms, struggled forward in this manner until they reached the altar. Behind the Church of Los Angeles, there was an outside chapel where holy water filled two stone basins. Worshippers went there to bless themselves after they had prayed in the church. They were joined by a homeless man who came in search of water to bathe himself. To my surprise, he calmly stripped off his shirt and proceeded to wash his upper body in the holy water. No one seemed to mind. They ignored his splashing, plunged their own hands into the water, and crossed themselves.

In Chiang Mai, Thailand, worshippers walked alongside their temple ringing a series of bells, one-by-one. The bells hung at waist height in a row along one wall. I was told that ringing the bells attracted the attention of the holy spirits residing in the temple. Similarly, in Osaka, Japan, I observed a grandmother clapping her hands together, while her little grandson watched and imitated her. They were standing in front of a series of stone altars in a courtyard, and the grandmother was teaching her protégé how to attract the gods, much like those worshippers ringing their bells in Chiang Mai.

In Mandalay, Burma, I wandered off by myself to explore an altar on the backside of a beautiful temple. The altar area was deserted, and it was so peaceful and serene, I hesitated to return to the main courtyard. The temple was surrounded by fields of rice with footpaths dissecting the crops in random squares. I noticed an elderly woman striding towards me along one of the footpaths and stopped to watch her. She entered the shrine, sank to her knees on the marble floor, and started to fervently chant a series of prayers in front of a stone image of Buddha. It was a Kodak moment, made more so by the fact that she never once looked in my direction. I was a ghost to her, an apparition that was not part of her world. Like the woman I had observed praying in Tibet, she was so enveloped in her spiritual universe, she didn't know that I existed.

In Congonhas, Brazil, a remarkable artist, Aleijadinho, also known as the Little Cripple, created a striking series of sculptures based on the stations of the cross. Each station was housed in a small building, and together, they told the story of Christ's crucifixion in a most dramatic manner. The sculptures led me up a hill to the Sanctuary, a whitewashed church built in the Baroque style where more than a dozen statues portraying Moses and other biblical figures stood guard like silent sentinels. What made Aleijadinho's work so special was his crippled condition. He couldn't use his hands, so his tools had to be strapped to his wrists. It was a lifetime project of devotion and love.

As I studied the stations, I was reminded of those small chapels I had seen at the Kumbum Stupa in Gyantse. Other images came to mind, as well, including images of people I had seen praying so passionately around the world. The images and the religious beliefs may have differed, but the message was pretty much the same: a spiritual order existed whose power determined the destiny of Mankind.

Here are a few more of those images.

Many years ago, I visited a temple in Taiwan where an old woman sat in the courtyard under the protection of an overhanging roof while a rainstorm thrummed overhead. She was tossing prayer sticks onto a table much like a game of pick-up sticks. Each time she tossed the sticks, she carefully studied how they had fallen, then chanted a series of prayers from a small book she held in her free hand. She repeated the process a dozen times or more under the flickering light of two burning candles that fought off the gloom surrounding her. Nearby, a temple sweeper sheltered himself from the rain and leaned on his broom, watching and nodding his head to the cadence of the woman's voice.

In Japan, people visit shrines to purchase fortunes that are written on small pieces of paper. Fortunes that are not favorable are tied like ribbons to one of several wires strung between two poles. It is believed that tying the bad fortune in this manner will negate the disappointing forecast. At the sanctuary I visited, so many poor fortunes had been purchased, the wires couldn't hold them all. The fortunes had spread like freshly fallen snow until they covered the nearby bushes and the low-hanging branches of two trees.

I have already described the beauty of St. Basil's church in Moscow, and St. Marks in Venice. There have been many others that have captured my fancy as well: the Duomo in Florence, Italy; the Uspensky Cathedral in Helsinki, Finland; the Aya Sofya in Istanbul, Turkey; and the Cathedral of Saints Stanislaw and Waclaw in Cracow, Poland, to name a few.

There is one cathedral that stands out in my memories in a very special way: the Notre Dame Cathedral in Paris. Its location along the Seine River is poetic, and its flying buttresses make it look as though it might take wing. But it isn't Notre Dame's physical aspects that make it so special. It's the three special images I found inside.

The first was a priest who sat in one of the side-rooms along the main hall. He was hunched over a desk and reading his bible by the light of a tiny lamp. Above his head, three stained-glass windows radiated a multitude of colors into the room. The priest's bald head and rotund figure reminded me of Friar Tuck in search of Robin Hood. Voices echoed around him. Feet shuffled. People coughed. None of this bothered the priest. He was as oblivious to the outside world as that woman I watched praying at the temple in Mandalay, Burma.

The second image captured a craftsman working in the rear of the Cathedral. He was down on his hands and knees restoring a section of flooring that dated back centuries. His hand movements were swift and sure, yet he worked with great care. He was tucked away from sight, and I might not have seen him at all except for a beam of light shining down from a window high overhead. It was as though the beam was lighting his way and blessing his work.

The third image was as unexpected as it was pleasurable. I was wandering through the Cathedral's vast, main room when a choir of boys and girls suddenly filed in and lined up in orderly rows in front of the choir master. The choir master raised his arms, and the choir began to sing. Their hymns resonated off the surrounding stone walls until every niche was filled with young tenor and soprano voices.

On a lighter note, I once observed four nuns standing in the main aisle of the church in Rottenbuch, Germany. They were admiring the brilliant ceiling frescoes and elaborate statuary soaring above the altar just like any tourist. It was one of those Bavarian churches I mentioned previously, and it was evident that the nuns were as enthralled with the artwork as I was. When they left the church, they proceeded directly to the souvenir shop around the corner, and just like any other group of tourists, they purchased post cards. I asked them to hold up their cards so that I could take their picture with them. All four held up the same card!

Enough about churches. Let's travel back to Tibet, where prayer wheels are used to spread enlightenment and blessings around the world. It's a common sight to see monks and worshippers twirling small prayer wheels as they walk. The wheel is shaped like a barrel that has been attached to the end of a round, wooden handle. A weighted chain dangles from the top of the barrel, and when the chain is spun in a clockwise direction, the barrel spins as well. Inside the barrel are prayers written on paper. Tibetans believe spinning the prayer wheels releases the prayers and spreads their spiritual messages of purity and wisdom into the world. Much larger prayer wheels are fastened in rows outside the monasteries so that people can spin them with their hands as they walk past and set the prayers free. Since Tibetans are Buddhists, they believe in reincarnation. By turning these prayer wheels, they expect to earn merits towards their next life.

Tibet also has many prescribed routes, called Lingkors, that circle specific monasteries. Tibetans circumambulate these routes while praying, always in a clockwise direction. One of the best known is the lingkor in Lhasa which circles the great Jokhang Monastery in Barkor Square. Here, pilgrims file in an endless procession around the outside of the monastery. An additional Lingkor can also be found inside the monastery that circles the main altar. Each completed circuit around the lingkor earns merits towards the next life.

Travel a few miles outside of Lhasa, and you will discover the Serra Monastery, where many of Tibet's Buddhist texts are printed and published. It is also a teaching monastery, and every afternoon a strange sight unfolds in a courtyard called the Debating Garden. Dozens of young monks gather there to debate what they have learned from that day's lessons at the Serra Je College, located within the monastery's walls.

The day I visited, I was greeted by the low din of debating voices swelling over the courtyard's walls. Inside, I found dozens of monks seated on the cold, hard ground with their maroon robes wrapped around them for warmth. An equal number of monks stood over them shouting their interpretations of the day's lessons. Each standing monk emphasized a point of discussion by raising one leg to waist level, slapping his hands together, and stomping his foot on the ground. The result was a vivid scene of organized chaos! Robes whipped and fluttered in the frosty air as the standing students stomped their feet again and again. Shouting voices and veils of dust permeated the courtyard. The seated monks attempted to resist this aggressive onslaught and to defend their own interpretations as best they could.

Fair was fair, however, and after awhile, the seated monks changed places and roles with their aggressors. Now, it was *their* turn to slap their hands and stomp their feet while they shouted at the monks seated before them. The debates raged in this manner for two hours.

I heard voices of a different sort one morning in Bhutan, murmuring voices that reminded me of water spilling over rocks in a stream. I had stayed the night in an old palace in Mongar, and the meager light creeping into my room the next morning told me it was still quite early. At first, I couldn't decide what was causing the murmurs that woke me. Was I dreaming? Had some wayward spirits invaded my bed? No, I realized, the sound came from chanting voices, most likely from the nearby monastery. I rose quickly and threw on three layers of warm clothes. It may have been mid-summer, but the morning air could sting the skin with the bite of a hundred frozen whips. I knew something special was happening, however, so I hurried outside and immersed myself in the morning's frosty air without hesitation.

When I entered the monastery's courtyard, I discovered dozens of young monks chanting morning prayers from well-worn manuscripts. Some sat by themselves along the railings ringing the second floor walkway. Others shared a book between them. However, most of the voices seemed to be coming from inside a modest, wooden building in the center of the courtyard, so I took off my shoes and ascended a steep flight of stairs to the monastery's second floor. There, I discovered a room filled with young initiates sitting on the floor and chanting. Curious eyes and shy smiles greeted me, but none stopped their rhythmic serenades. There were no stomping feet or shouting voices there, nor dust rising from the wood floors. Serenity replaced the jostling scenes I had witnessed in that debating garden in Tibet. A sense of peace and calm prevailed. Yet the goal was the same: to learn the intricate teachings of Buddha based on the Four Noble Truths and the Eightfold Path.

Let's end this chapter with a spiritual encounter that took place at the Tsurpu Monastery in Tibet. Tsurpu was the home of the 17th Karmapa, a twelve-year-old boy god who, in the absence of the Dalai Lama, was considered the most important religious leader in the country. I was on my way to meet him and to pay him homage. It was a journey that required several-hours-drive by car on something that was not so much a road as a teeth rattling series of rocks and cavities that made normal progress nearly impossible. The car banged and thumped its way along as my driver maneuvered over and around these obstacles; I sat in the back and gripped the seat with both hands in a futile effort to keep from banging my head off the ceiling.

We entered a narrow valley and began to pass tiny villages. Goats, pigs, and yaks roamed freely along the lower slopes of the surrounding mountains. Mounds of wheat stood in the shape of golden igloos in the fields. Peasants pitched the wheat onto wooden carts, filling each cart until the grain cascaded over the sides. I could feel the altitude changing as we climbed steadily into a range of mountains that seemed determined to block our path. I estimated our altitude at over fourteen thousand, an estimate that was confirmed when a thin layer of snow began to appear in irregular patterns in the surrounding fields. The spring-like morning I had left behind in Lhasa had turned into a bone-chilling, sleet-gray day. The snow line crept relentlessly closer, until the entire valley was blanketed in a winter-white coat. Winter came early to this bleak valley, if it ever left at all.

The valley narrowed even more, and the mounds of wheat were replaced by hundreds of yaks wandering through the snow foraging for food. At last, a series of prayer flags could be seen stretched across a frozen stream and the Tsurpu Monastery revealed itself tucked against a hillside of tortured rocks.

Men's voices could be heard booming from the monastery's Assembly Hall when I entered the courtyard. A brief flight of stone steps led me to the hall where rows of monks sat on pillows and chanted their prayers. Seated on a raised platform at the far end of the hall was the boy I had come to see. He wasn't much more than a child, but his regal bearing, dark, piercing gaze, and flared nose gave him the countenance of a young king.

There was a great deal of controversy with China about how the 17th Karmapa was chosen. He had been originally selected by the Chinese who intended to use his selection to undermine the Dalai Lama's spiritual control over the Tibetans, but his name was slipped out of Tibet in time for the Dalai Lama to proclaim him the 17th Karmapa prior to China's declaration. By regaining control of the selection process, the Dalai Lama maintained his supreme position of authority among the Tibetans, and the Chinese government was furious.

Considering the drama surrounding the boy, I suppose I shouldn't have been surprised to see the tight security protecting him. Following prayers, I stood in line with several dozen pilgrims who wanted to pay homage to the boy god, but before any of us could ascend the stairs to the room where he waited, we had to pass through a metal detector similar to those used at airports. It was also necessary to leave my camera bag and equipment on a table downstairs. The Tibetans were taking no chances.

My guide gave me a white, silk scarf, and when my turn came, I stepped forward and laid it on the pile of scarves offered by the Tibetans before me. The boy sat unmoving in a lotus position on a raised platform that put him at eye level. He stared at me with silent eyes that neither blinked nor moved. I was one of only a handful of westerners in line that day, but if he noticed, it didn't register on his face. His mood seemed pensive, as if he was lost in thought and refused to be distracted by all the fuss around him.

There's an ironic ending to this story. Less than a year after I paid homage to him, the 17th Karmapa fled over the Himalayas, just as the Dalai Lama had done nearly forty years before him, and joined Tibet's most revered leader in exile. Like the Dalai Lama, the boy god had decided there was little he could do to help his countrymen by remaining in the country. It seemed a mature decision for someone so young, and it made me think back to his expression the day I met him. I know, now, that he carried a tremendous weight on his young shoulders, a weight that expressed itself in those silent eyes.

A few years later, I learned that the 17th Karmapa planned to visit San Luis Obispo, California, to bless the area. What an unexpected surprise! SLO was just up the road from our home, so Fe and I went to see him. Once again, I stood in line with a scarf which I presented to him. Only this time, those around me were westerners, not Tibetans, and when I presented my scarf I was able to tell the young man about our previous encounter. The 17th Karmapa now spoke reasonably good English and told me he was pleased to see me again. His look told me he hadn't escaped his burden by leaving Tibet. He traveled the world telling the Tibetans' story and keeping his country alive in peoples' memories. If anything, he had probably added to the weight on his shoulders.

# CHAPTER TWELVE
## *FAVORITE THESE AND THATS*

Chemainus is a delightful town found just north of Victoria on Vancouver Island, Canada, where local artists have painted brilliant motifs on the sides of buildings to commemorate the history and character of the place. When you arrive, you are given a map, and there are painted footsteps on the sidewalks to guide you from one mural to the next. All-in-all, it makes for a charming day's walk, but what made it particularly special for me was an incident that occurred during my explorations. A native woman walking in front of me suddenly decided to hoist her two-year-old boy onto her shoulders, not realizing that the boy's pants were being pulled down in the process. The boy's bare rear end was left for the world to see. His older brother was particularly pleased with this development. He walked along merrily whacking his little brother on his exposed butt with his hand. It made a memorable photograph.

I think the most wonderful thing we can bring home from our world travels isn't souvenirs. It is memories. Memories of a special place or moment, like that little boy on his mother's shoulders. But picking a favorite is tough, not only because so many places and events are special, but because there are a variety of elements to consider: people, scenery, history, unusual events, personal experiences, and so forth. How do you choose just one? A little trick that helps me is to sort my favorite memories into different categories. That can only take me so far, however. There are often dozens of memories that I could pick for any one category, but at least the process of categorizing makes things more manageable. Naturally, all of my choices speak to me in some special way. Sharing a few of mine might be a fun way to end this book, and I hope they will spark special memories of your favorites, as well.

**Favorite Sunrise:** This one's easy. During my two photographic journeys through Tibet, I spent a total of five nights in Lhasa. Each morning I rose before dawn and walked approximately two miles to the foot of the Potala, a sacred thirteen story building that rose on a hill facing the holy city like a great battle ship ready to be launched at sea. Before the Chinese invaded Tibet, the Potala was a combined monastery, winter residence for the Dalai Lama, and center of government. It was said to house over ten thousand shrines and more than two hundred thousand Buddha images. Across the street, a smaller hill, called Chokpori, stared back at this imposing structure. I discovered a footpath there that led up the hill to a lookout point where I could photograph the Potala as the sun struggled to free itself from behind the mountain range to my right. The result was a series of striking images, but my favorite was one I captured in hazy light before the sun had cleared the horizon. Smoke from cooking fires and the misty blue light of dawn produced a timeless setting that transported the Potala back to an era before foreigners invaded the holy city.

The first invader was the British army led by Colonel Younghusband in 1904. Then came the Chinese army, which arrived in 1951. Unlike the British, they never left, and today

Lhasa looks like any other Chinatown, festooned with Chinese signs as far as the eye can see and overwhelmed by multi-storied buildings designed to obscure the Potala and reduce its importance. On this one particular morning, as the sun fought its daily battle with the nearby mountains, I stared at the mist-enshrouded Potala sitting on its hilltop, and I saw the simple village that had once surrounded this enduring symbol of Tibetan independence and culture. That was the Lhasa I would always remember . . . the one that rose in the mists of a Tibetan sunrise.

**Favorite Sunset:** Paris, France. On this particular trip, Paris was only a stopover. Fe and I planned to spend the night at an airport hotel before continuing on to Frankfurt the next morning, but we arrived early enough to hop a train into the city for dinner. The sun was setting when we emerged from the underground station on the Champs Elysees, and we both caught our breaths and stopped to stare at the fiery red ball as it slowly descended towards the Arc de Triomphe.

I used to teach a class on travel photography, and something I emphasized was the importance of always carrying your camera with you, no matter the time of day or the circumstances. Of course, everybody has cell phones with built-in cameras, now, but the day I saw that sunset in Paris, cameras were still somewhat cumbersome beasts hanging from shoulder straps or stuffed in camera bags.

Fortunately, I practiced what I preached that day, and with cameras in hand, I hurried to the middle of the Champs Elysees in time to watch and photograph the flaming sun as it dropped like the New Years Eve ball in Times Square right through the center of the Arc. For a few precious seconds, a dazzling spectacle of orange-red hues lit up the Arc's graceful archway, then the fiery ball quickly slid from view. It was already transforming itself into a golden sunrise somewhere else on the world's horizon, perhaps in Tibet.

**Favorite Rock:** After my description of Mont-St.-Michel, you might think that would be my favorite rock, and it was close. But there's another that I found even more exhilarating: Ayers Rock in Australia. I always thought that anyone who would travel hundreds of miles across a landscape that consisted of hardscrabble, harsh temperatures (think hot), and ostriches sticking their heads in the sand, just to see a rock in the middle of the desert, had either run out of places to go and things to see or was suffering from severe sleep deprivation. I couldn't imagine anything more futile, yet there I was doing exactly that . . . and enjoying every minute of the experience.

After driving for hours across the flat, unyielding outback, Ayers Rock suddenly appeared on the horizon. It looked more like a figment of my imagination than sandstone and granite. Its steep walls were shaped like a very long camel's hump, and they leapt out of the ground like a rabbit pulled from a magician's hat. Pock-marked walls, deep crevices, hidden pools of water, and a surface that seemed to shift colors with its moods were all part of its charm.

There are a few things worth knowing about Ayers Rock. Many come to climb it, but there's no trail leading to the top, only a steep granite face that will quickly discourage those who are not in reasonably good shape. A chain dangling from a series of poles inserted in the ground provides handholds for those who need them, but the real challenge is to make the ascent on you own. The face is exposed to severe winds, however, that can sweep across it with enough force to blow you right off the rock if you're not careful. I learned later that a lot of people had died climbing the rock, either from falls or heart attacks. If you do reach the top, the next challenge is to sign the registry book, but the registry book isn't found there. It's about a city block away, and to reach it, you must clamber over a badly eroded surface filled with sink holes that require you to run down one side and up the other without the benefit of handholds. The trail you must follow has broken arms and legs written all over it! The descent is no picnic either. It's so steep that by the time you reach the bottom, your legs feel like jelly.

There is just one small problem with climbing Ayers Rock. The aborigines ask you not to do it. They call the rock Uluru, and to them it's a very spiritual place. In fact, the climbing route is considered a sacred path. This wasn't common knowledge when Fe and I were there in the mid-1980s, and many tourists are still unaware of the issue today, until they get there. Considering how far they've come, many still climb, but some do not.

For me, the highlight wasn't so much the climb as the sunset, when the sandstone and granite surfaces of Ayers rock change more shades of crimson than I did ordering that duck l'orange in France. Large crowds gather to watch and photograph the changing colors as the rock shifts from sandy loam to brilliant rust red to printers-ink purple. A great many people gather to watch the sunset, making it difficult to take a photograph without heads or people in it. If you want a clear shot, you must clamber several hundred yards out into the hardscrabble and brush. The effort is worth it, but be careful not to jump in front of other peoples' cameras.

**Favorite Hotel:** The Sheraton Mirage in Port Douglas, Australia. This was a brand new luxury property when we arrived there, and we were delighted to immerse ourselves in its glorious swimming pools, spas, flowing bathrobes, and exquisite restaurants for a few days. We needed a bit of pampering after that climb up Ayers Rock. Port Douglas is about an hour north of Cairns, so we spent our days boating and snorkeling around the Great Barrier Reef. Then we returned to our hotel for a luxurious bubble bath and a gourmet dinner.

By now, you have probably guessed there's more to the story. We arrived the same afternoon that we climbed Ayers Rock. At dinner time we tried to walk down a short flight of stairs from our hotel room to the dining area, only to discover that our calf muscles had twisted into knots from the morning's ordeal. We couldn't walk down the stairs! I was thinking about getting down on my hands and knees and crawling, until we discovered that if we turned around, we could walk down the stairs backwards. I won't bother to describe the strange stares we got from other guests as they walked past us.

But that's only half the story. The tour guide with whom I was working had decided we should enjoy the hour's drive between Cairns and Port Douglas by limousine, so we arrived at the hotel in grand style. When we checked out a few days later the limo had not yet returned to pick us up, so I helped Fe put our bags by the curb, and she waited there while I went back to settle our bill. Several people were already standing around the broad, curved hotel entrance waiting for the bus that would ferry them back to Cairns. Some were guests, but most were maids and other hotel staff who were going off duty for the day.

The rest of this story is Fe's, because I wasn't there. I was still at the checkout counter. First, you have to get a mental image of Fe dressed in casual jeans and a simple blouse standing near the cleaning ladies and other hotel staff. Next, picture a businessman in a tailored suit who stepped to the curb beside her, followed by a bellman carrying his bags. The businessman eyed Fe for a few moments, then started to chat with her. Fe learned that he had been enjoying a brief respite from a business trip, and he was now waiting for a taxi to take him back to Cairns for a meeting. It quickly became apparent that he thought she was part of the hired help waiting for the bus, and he invited her to share his cab at no expense back to Cairns. Fe thanked him, but said she already had made arrangements. Then, right on cue from stage left, what should appear but our limousine! The driver pulled to the curb in front of Fe, popped the trunk, deposited our luggage, and held the back door open for her to get in. All the while, the businessman stood there in wide-eyed amazement. I wish I could've seen his expression, but by the time I got there, his taxi had come and gone and I'd missed the whole thing.

**Favorite Conversation:** I'm bunching a few Aussie favorites together. Before Fe and I went to Ayers Rock, we visited Alice Springs. This was a relatively small and very quaint town when we were there, with a number of colorful locals, including aborigines who got quite upset if you tried to take their picture without tipping them first. Their life was rather sad. They had no jobs and lived on government dole, much of which was used to purchase alcohol. In that regard, they reminded me of the Eskimos I had seen years before in Anchorage, Alaska. Both native populations became easily addicted to alcohol because their bodies couldn't assimilate the stuff. Most of the local aborigines spent their afternoons drinking down in the dry creek bed that ran through the town. There were a few, however, who were productive artists, and we saw some amazing artwork based on their ancient folklore and customs.

Okay, back to the conversation. We took a taxi from the airport to our hotel, a drive of about fifteen minutes, and struck up a conversation with our very friendly driver. Actually, he was the one who talked and we listened . . . for fifteen minutes . . . all the way to the hotel. That would've been okay, but there was a problem. We couldn't understand a word he said! I thought I was back in France ordering duck l'orange. He was speaking English, but with such a heavy, outback accent, it might as well have been aborigine. Fe and I uh-huh-ed from time to time to let him know we were listening, and he happily blabbed away about God knows what until we arrived at the front entrance to our hotel.

**Favorite Waterfalls:** That would be the horseshoe-shaped Iguassu Falls I mentioned in Chapter Four that are found at the point in South America where Brazil, Argentina, and Paraguay meet. All two hundred and seventy-five of them! Iguassu combines the sheer power of the world's other great falls with delicate veiled falls and dozens of rainbows. They stretch for miles along the borders of Brazil and Argentina. Platforms have been strategically placed a few feet above the river so that you can cross the river on foot to the edge of the most powerful fall, Devil's Throat.

When Fe and I visited the falls, however, the Iguassu River had recently thrown a giant temper tantrum and wiped out most of the platforms on Argentina's side. One small platform remained directly above Devil's Throat, but the only way to reach it was by boat. You're probably imagining a nice big boat with an anchor and maybe some lines securing it to the mainland. Uh, uh. This boat wasn't much larger than a dugout canoe, and the only thing keeping it from being swept over the falls was a small, outboard engine that sputtered and coughed more often than not. A person had to be crazy to take that thing anywhere near Devil's Throat, but that's exactly what we did. Was it worth it? In a word, yes! When we finally reached the postage-stamp sized platform that stood on the edge of the precipice, we looked straight down into the thundering jaws of Devil's Throat. I can tell you that the falls lived up to its name. It was a massive avalanche of water that swept everything in its path to destruction. I couldn't help thinking about the flimsy outboard motor on the launch that had carried us there and praying that it wouldn't fail us on the return trip. Otherwise, we would be "swimming with the fishes."

**Favorite Square:** The Plac Zamkowy in front of the Royal Castle at the foot of the Royal Route in Warsaw, Poland, but not for the reasons you might think. The nearby Old Town Square is really more interesting and picturesque, and I can think of far grander squares around the world. (I previously mentioned the square with five cathedrals in the Kremlin in Moscow.) What made the Plac Zamkowy so special was the display of "Buddy Bears" standing on their hind legs in rows around the square. Each of these life-size bears represented a different country, and each bear was painted with scenes and images by artists that portrayed that country's character in some meaningful way. The United States bear, for example, was dressed like the statue of liberty. The Cuban bear had a big, Havana cigar sticking out of its mouth. One of the African bears displayed colorful costumes and hunting images.

The idea behind the Buddy Bears was to prompt world unity and peace, and the display was being shipped from country to country. Its journey just happened to coincide with ours to Plac Zamkowy square.

**Favorite Story:** The first time I visited Hong Kong, it was still a British Colony and the New Territories were filled with duck farms and rice paddies, not the skyscraper cities of today. Twenty thousand British worked and lived in Hong Kong, many in life styles that would have been well beyond their means back home. I had the pleasure of meeting one of these expatriated gentlemen, Robert Morris, at the Kowloon Cricket Club. He pointed out that things were not always as tranquil as they appeared. One day in 1967 stood out vividly in his mind. There had been a series of Chinese labor demonstrations and riots on the Kowloon mainland for months, and they had become quite political, with Communist trade unions hiring demonstrators to foment the unrest. The protests finally spilled over onto the island of Hong Kong where many of the British resided and where the financial and government centers were located. On that fateful day, rioters confronted police around the area of the Hong Kong Hilton. It just so happened that Morris' lawn bowling team from the Kowloon Cricket Club was in the midst of a match that day with the bowlers of the Hilton Club on the playing field directly across the street from the hotel.

"There we were," he recalls, "in the middle of our match, and the first thing we know our green is surrounded by these bloody Chinese demonstrators. We knew they wanted to come on the field and do us harm, but the orderly appearance of our manner as we bowled seemed to hold them back. So we really couldn't do much else, could we? We bloody well went on and finished our game.

"After the match was over, we skipped tea and went straight to the showers. Somehow, I took a little longer than the others, and when I left I was alone. As I headed down to the ferry to return to Kowloon I suddenly realized that I was surrounded by these demonstrators. I thought, 'My God, I'm done for,' but they paid me no attention at all. It was after five, you see, and since they had only been hired to demonstrate until five o'clock they were finished for the day and going home, same as me."

**Favorite River:** The Amazon River. Not the place to go to see castles or palaces along the shore, but if you want to witness nature flexing its muscles, this is the place to be. I've already described the incredible torrents of rain that fall along the river. There is so much rain during the rainy season that the Amazon rises some forty feet. My first trip was at the end of the rainy season, and I was able to float in a canoe among the forest's giant tree tops while I tried to imagine the forest hidden in the water beneath my feet. My next trip to the Amazon was during the dry season, so I finally got to see the trees from top to bottom. They towered over my head with so much foliage, their canopy shut out much of the sunlight. There was amazingly little plant life at ground level due to the lack of sunlight. Most of the plants and the majority of wildlife lived up in the trees.

The entire length of the river is estimated to be between 3,900 miles and 4,200 miles. Yet from its origins to its mouth in the North Atlantic Ocean, it drains less than 400 feet. That's less than one inch for every mile. Water in a bath tub drains faster. That's why its surface often looks more like a giant glass mirror than the world's mightiest river. The effect can be quite stunning. Clouds and jungle are reflected so perfectly, it's often difficult to tell where the reflection ends, and the sky begins.

**Favorite Lodgings:** Yes, I know that I've already discussed my favorite hotel, but this is different and a perfect follow-up to my favorite river. Fe and I stayed overnight in a lodge on the Amazon River that floated during the rainy season, and sat on land during the dry season. We had the pleasure of staying there when it was floating. It was firmly secured to the shore by long cables, but we needed a boat to ferry us back and forth. The lodge was roughhewn but quite comfortable, with four bedrooms. After dark, dozens of holler monkeys sang to us from the nearby trees, and other strange noises went bump in the night. It was an exhilarating experience.

The best was yet to come, however. I awoke in the middle of the night and decided to wander out on-deck. The sky was overflowing with brilliant pinpoints of light cast by millions of stars that spilled endlessly out of the heavens and into the still waters beneath my feet. The effect was seamless; I couldn't tell where the stars ended and their reflections began. It was like standing in the middle of a fireworks display that had become frozen in time. Words like "dazzling" and "overwhelming" didn't begin to describe the effect. The only image I could think of that might capture the moment would be that of an astronaut floating in space.

**Favorite Region:** Tuscany, Italy. There is something magical about Tuscany: its rolling hills layered in early morning mists; its afternoon sunlight dancing among puffy clouds across Chianti vineyards and ancient walled towns that seem to pop up on every hilltop; and its historic cities scattered across the landscape in a plethora of church steeples, watch towers, fortress walls, and Roman ruins.

Florence alone would make this region special. There is so much artwork, the city reeks of the stuff. At the Medici Palace alone, it's possible to view over four hundred years of paintings, statues, and tapestries. The Pitti Palace offers more artwork and a dazzling maze of exquisite gardens. Then there is the Duomo. Originally designed to be the world's largest Roman Catholic Church, its dome rises above Florence's skyline in the shape of a giant ice cream cone and is rivaled only by the church's Campanile di Giotto, a slender bell tower which, from a distance, gives the appearance of a delicate index finger pointed to the heavens. Facing the Duomo is the squat, octagonal baptistry, which might go unnoticed with the Duomo and Campanile for neighbors, but for its sculptured and gilded bronze doors. The door's ten panels depict scenes from the bible in such intricacy, many believe they are the most beautiful doors in the world. If I had a favorite doors category, that would be it.

Florence's treasures are endless, and no visit to this fabled city is complete without a stroll across Ponte Vecchio Bridge, a collage of shuttered windows and extravagant jewelry and goldsmith shops that spans the River Arno. The jewelry is magnificent, but the real pleasure is observing the span from the river bank. From that viewpoint, the backs of the shops hang over the river like Monopoly pieces held in place by chewing gum. The River Arno threw its own temper tantrum, in 1966 and nearly destroyed the gilded doors from the Duomo's baptistery. Some of the panels were feared lost, but all were eventually recovered. It took the patience and talents of specially trained artisans to restore them to their golden brilliance.

But enough about Florence. There is so much more to Tuscany than one city. In fact, there is a city close by that in many ways rivals Florence for its panache. I'm referring to Siena, which is not only Florence's rival but its altar ego. Siena is one giant time warp. Step onto its cobbled streets and you journey back to the middle ages. That's how little things have changed over the centuries. You will discover fortress walls, statues of angels and saints carved into stone niches, and bell towers galore. And you must explore on foot. Like Venice, Siena doesn't allow cars inside its city limits. All the main streets lead to the Piazza del Campo, a red-bricked plaza of grand proportions that fans out in the middle of the city. The plaza is shaped in the fashion of a giant pizza that slopes away from the restaurants ringing the back of the square and down to the Chapel of the Virgin at its base. Gaggles of tourists arrive there each day to dine in the outdoor cafes and bask on the sun-drenched bricks. They reminded me of Canadian geese that had flown south for the winter.

All that changes when the ancient horserace called the Palio is running. The race takes place in the plaza itself. Family clans prepare their horses for months in advance, and alliances are formed to better a horse's odds. On the day of the race, the horses are actually led into a church to be blessed, and fifty thousand spectators fill the middle of the plaza. The race is over in not much more than a minute, but the drama and plotting that precede it are legendary.

There is so much more, it's hard to stop talking about Tuscany. Suffice at this point to briefly mention the Leaning Tower of Pisa whose gravity defying tilt has mesmerized visitors for centuries, the Monte Oliveto Maggiore monastery with fresco panels depicting the life of St. Benedict, hilltop towns called Sovana and Volterra, San Gimignano which once bristled with seventy-two towers (fourteen remain), and Pistoia, once a violent medieval town where the manufacture of small firearms in the 16th century gave birth to the word "pistol."

**Favorite Historical Moment:** The Berlin Wall coming down. The year was 1989, and Fe and I were on a train headed for East Germany with little idea what to expect. The Wall separating East and West Germany had fallen, but we didn't know who was in charge. The East German consulate had informed us before leaving the U.S. that we still needed visas and a hotel reservation to enter the country. We had neither. Our goal was Berlin, but as we approached the East German border, we tensed and waited. Would our train ride into history be aborted? Would we be greeted by those feared East German guards who would remove us from the train and send us packing back to the West? Or would we be embraced by freedom? To our immense relief, the train never missed a click or a clack, and we hurtled into the abyss that had for decades been defined as a political fortress called the Iron Curtain.

That probably sounds a bit melodramatic, but in 1989 freedom was still an unrealized dream for a whole generation of East Germans, and those of us trying to peek over the wall from the West couldn't imagine how unarmed citizens could ever wrest control away from the East German secret police, known as the Stasi. It didn't take long, however, to see how badly the Communist regime had managed things. Our train rumbled past the rusted-out hulks of manufacturing plants with broken windows and twisted metal lying in weed-infested yards. The buildings looked more like the abandoned remnants of some WWII bombing raid than functioning factories, yet people were working in them. It made us realize just how badly East Germany's economy had faded in the face of global competition, computerized production, and the flow of investments and new technologies around the world.

When we rolled into Berlin, we saw a few East German

soldiers still guarding the war memorial near the Berlin Wall, but the city had already been abandoned to the West. People were celebrating with picks, hammers, and any other tools they could find to chip away at the Wall that had barricaded them from the West for so many decades. Brightly colored graffiti covered the Wall with the symbols and words of freedom, and thousands of people were merrily whacking away at it. Gypsies had set up sidewalk shops in front of the Brandenburg Gate to sell Russian military hats and uniforms as souvenirs. The clothing had been sold to the gypsies by Russian soldiers who were no longer being paid. The infamous crossing between East and West known as Check Point Charley stood deserted, its warning signs no longer deterring anyone and its inquisition rooms no longer instilling fear. In other parts of the city, secondary check points were already being bulldozed into history. Check Point Charley would soon follow.

**Unforgettable Memorials:** Favorite isn't the best word for this one, so I've changed it to unforgettable. Everywhere you travel in Greece, you will see memorials along the roadsides that mourn the loss of loved ones. The Greeks are very colorful and expressive people, who live and sometimes drink with an exuberance that carries over to their driving. The result is too many fatal accidents and too many memorials. They usually have glass windows. Inside, small shrines are displayed, often with pictures and other memorabilia of the lost family member. A cross or image of the Virgin Mary is nearly always included. Each one tells a story in poignant terms. One particularly eloquent monument displayed an unopened can of baby food and one tiny shoe.

**Favorite City:** Forbidden. The first time I saw the Forbidden City in Beijing, China, there was snow on the ground and hardly a tourist in sight. Sunlight was reflecting off the imperial rooftops, and I was surrounded by a timeless maze of palaces and courtyards. The city was considered the emperor's divine residence on earth, and ordinary people were forbidden to enter it. That ended with the last emperor, but I still felt privileged to be there. From my vantage point on the steps leading to the Hall of Supreme Harmony, it was possible to imagine the shuffle of servants' shoes on the stones as they hurried to do the emperor's bidding, the rattle of swords and armor worn by soldiers standing guard at each gate, the rustling silk dresses and painted faces of the ladies of the court, and the click-clack of horses' hooves echoing across the courtyards.

With a little imagination it was easy to grasp the magnificence of the place, but it was harder to appreciate its size. There were ninety palaces and courtyards alone, and nearly a thousand buildings. The grounds measured more than 175 acres. Who wouldn't have felt like a descendant from God when living there? And what wonderful names for everything: Hall of Heavenly Purity, Hall of Earthly Tranquility, Nine Dragon Wall, Palace of Tranquil Longevity, and the gates of Supreme Harmony and Heavenly Purity. The gates were guarded by bronze and golden lions. It was believed the lions scared away evil spirits or devil, which reminded me of the zigzag bridges in Shanghai that prevented evil spirits from reaching its famous tea house. How many evil spirits were there in these places, I wondered?

**Favorite Forest:** All of Finland. I had the opportunity to travel through much of Finland, and other than a few cities and towns located primarily in the southern portion of the country, mostly what I saw were trees. Birch trees to be exact, with a smattering of pines tossed in here and there. In fact, when people asked me to describe Finland, I told them *it was a country of birch trees interrupted by an occasional forest*. I got more than a few blank stares on that one. You had to have been there to truly understand what I meant. The exception was the lake district where the birch trees were interrupted by occasional lakes. Most of the lakes had one pair of swans that had taken up residence there. I learned the swans mated for life, so if only one was seen, it probably meant the other had died. Finland is a lovely country, by the way, especially if you like birch trees!

**Favorite Museum:** The Louvre. This one is a no-brainer for me. There are many great museums in the world: the Rijksmuseum in Amsterdam, Hermitage Museum in St. Petersburg, Egyptian Museum in Cairo, and Medici Palace in Florence to name a few. However, none can match the brilliance of the Louvre in Paris. It is simply the world's greatest museum in the world's greatest palace. It takes the better part of a day just to find your way around the place, and now that they have added the glass pyramid entrances, there's a futuristic touch, as well. There are three floors and three massive wings: the Sully, Denon, and Richelieu, covering everything from sculptures and paintings to Greek, Roman, Oriental, and Egyptian antiquities. There is one room in the Denon Wing, however, that just blows me away. It's filled with giant canvasses from the nineteenth century that portray such masterpieces as Delacroix's "The Death of Sardanapalus" and Geri Ault's "The Raft of the Medusa." I can sit and look at the paintings in that room for an hour or more.

**Favorite Road:** The Pralatenweg. This is a road in Bavarian Germany that consists of a loosely knit network of monasteries, cloisters, and churches dating back to the $8^{th}$ century. They are connected by a series of trails and roads which can be traveled by following little white signs with two blue staffs painted on them. Many of the roads permit auto traffic, but in some places only hiking and bicycling are allowed. Together, they form the Pralatenweg which begins in the town of Marktoberdorf and ends in Kochel. Along the way, ancient monasteries and churches in towns like Seeshaupt, Bernreid, Lechbruck, and Bobing await you. These are not your typical tourist destinations, but it's worth the trip to see the interiors of these places. Alters nestle among profusions of elaborate sculptures and paintings. Ceilings burst forth with rich, colorful frescoes depicting angels, saints, and biblical scenes. Golden pulpits rise above the pews.

Many wonderful details merge into a colorful collage of memories along the Pralatenweg. In Steingarden, an incredibly old bible rests on a stand by the altar. A wooden doorknob in Rottenbuch has the church's image carved on it. The small chapel behind the church in Poling sits in a cemetery filled with ornate tombstones. Inside the chapel, heavy, woolen blankets hang over the backs of the pews, attesting to the chill worshippers must endure in winter. In Benedicktbeuern, an alcove has been stuck onto the monastery's exterior wall, and a tiny creek flows under one wing of the building.

**Favorite Zen Garden:** Serenity is the perfect word to describe the Zen garden that I visited in Japan. A large bed of sand in the center of the garden had been meticulously raked into a spider web of lines encircling several small rocks and boulders. A handful of worshippers sat on a deck meditating and immersing themselves in the vista before them. I joined them, and after some minutes discovered that the sand and rocks had become transformed into a timeless world of clouds, deserts, and oceans. Spatial elements shifted, as well. I was no longer certain if the rocks were feet apart or miles away, whether I was looking at sand or a spiritual ocean. It all depended on where my vision transported me. I do not pretend to know about Zen philosophies, but I found the garden very spiritual.

**Favorite Monastery:** That would be Taktsang or Tiger's Nest in Bhutan, a monastery revered throughout the country. It was founded, according to legend, by Guru Rinpoche when he flew into Bhutan on the back of a tiger. He meditated in a cave carved by rain and snow into a sheer cliff overlooking the surrounding valleys, and that was where the monastery was built.

Reaching the monastery requires a very steep climb from 7,000 feet to 10,000 feet, not something for the feint of heart! The lower part of the trail follows footpaths through fields and forest. Midway up the mountain a small shrine with prayer wheels and flags greets you, and about the time that your breathing becomes labored and your legs lose their resolve, you reach an outlook where you can gaze across a great divide at the monastery clinging to its ledge along sheer granite walls less than a mile away. There is a snack stand with outdoor tables where you can rest and marvel at the spectacular setting. Many people end their trek there, but for those who are more adventurous, the trail continues through a forest covered in hanging moss and lichens, then up the tortuous ledge to the monastery itself.

The place creaked with age and history when I visited. Its calloused wood gate and protective walls had the blackened appearance of a stand of trees that had withstood the ravages of a fire. Which seems prophetic now. Within a year of my glorious, breathtaking climb to that revered sanctuary, fire did destroy the monastery and monks' quarters. It has since been rebuilt, but I cannot imagine it holds quite the same mysterious charm as before.

**Favorite Humorous Story:** I've already shared a favorite story, but what better way to end this chapter than with a humorous travel story? The person who told it to me swore it really happened, but to me it sounds a little far fetched. See what you think.

Two men were jogging on the beach at a Caribbean resort when they noticed a camera lying on a beach towel. The woman who owned it was cooling herself in the surf with her back turned to the beach. Without hesitation, one man scooped up the camera while the other dropped his bathing trunks. The first man quickly snapped two pictures of his friend's private parts and put the camera back on the beach towel. The trunks were pulled up, and the two men continued their jog along the beach. Now, here's the question you have to ask yourself. How in the world did that poor woman explain those two pictures to her husband or boyfriend, or to herself, for that matter, when she got home and downloaded her photographs?

# AFTERWORD

I hope you have enjoyed reading this travelogue as much as I have enjoyed writing it. Every story in the book is true, but I know this is only the tip of the travel iceberg. You undoubtedly have a funny story or two of your own. If you would like to share your funniest adventure in a one-page email with me, I would enjoy reading it. Please email me at gjsnider@sbcglobal.net. It would be fun to learn about your stories and to see what I have missed.

Travel is such a remarkable undertaking, so rich in personal experiences and so rewarding in the discovery of new places and cultures. Even when things go wrong . . . go wrong . . . go wrong, the rewards nearly always outweigh the disappointments. And I have invariably found that some of the best and funniest stories come from these unexpected trials. Just remember to "breathe in another language" and to enjoy the adventure, wherever it takes you. Personally, all this talk about travel has me ready to go again. But first, I had better check my passport to make sure it isn't out of date!

Bon voyage.

CPSIA information can be obtained at www.ICGtesting.com
Printed in the USA
BVOW08s0854270416

445815BV00001B/33/P